Fishbourne

Fishbourne

A Roman Palace and its Garden

Barry Cunliffe

7 Color Plates
86 Monochrome Plates
40 Line Drawings

THE JOHNS HOPKINS PRESS · BALTIMORE

Published in the United States of America
by the Johns Hopkins Press, Baltimore, Maryland 21218

Library of Congress Catalog Card Number 79–139850

Copyright © 1971 in London, England, by Thames and Hudson Ltd.

First published in 1971

Printed in Switzerland

Contents

Preface

The great building which Professor Barry Cunliffe has excavated with consummate skill at Fishbourne in Sussex during nine arduous seasons and here presents in readily comprehensible form is unique amongst the vestiges of Roman Britain. Historically it throws a new light upon the social and political policy of Roman imperialism in action during the sensitive half-century following the Claudian invasion in AD 43. And in so doing it has yielded to impeccable excavation a palace on a metropolitan scale, covering a nuclear ten acres and extending beyond these into vistas at present unplanned. Above all, it goes as far as archaeology may be expected normally to take us into the mind and functioning of an outstanding personality hitherto familiar to us only by a shadowy though intriguing style and title.

'King Cogidubnus, Legate of the Emperor in Britain.' In his honoured old age we can now approach him with a proper deference through the propylaeum on the eastern side of his palace, cross a central garden laid out with something like a Louis Quatorze finesse, and ascend the steps into an apsidal hall-of-audience where he awaits us. A 'quisling'? Maybe. But I like the apologia with which Professor Cunliffe supports his Celtic kinglet in Roman guise. Can it really be that Cogidubnus sprang suddenly from pre-Roman squalor into the imposed sophistication of palatial Rome? Or was he already when enthroned in some sense a foster-child of Rome, deliberately prepared by youthful habit to assume the splendours and conventions of civilized environment? Why was he chosen by the conqueror for explicit recognition not only as King but also as Legate or Lieutenant of the Emperor himself? Already there had been no little trafficking on occasion between the Celtic rulers of the fringe and the Roman world. In AD 7 the king of the Atrebates, whose territories lay to the north-westwards of the Chichester region, had fled to Rome in search of help during tribal disputation. On the eve of the Claudian invasion his younger brother and successor, King Verica, followed suit. The neighbourly relationships of the coastal tribe or sept over which Cogidubnus was to rule are less clear; they were no doubt increasingly precarious as the anti-Roman Catuvellauni to the north of the Thames pressed southwards towards the coast. The context might be regarded as ripe for yet another sibling from the family of Verica or his kind to find refuge, hospitality and indoctrination at Rome. The author cites an analogy from the German frontier: the young prince Italicus, nephew of the German patriot Arminius, born and educated in Rome where his mother was a hostage, and subsequently sent out by Claudius to rule his own ancestral tribe. As another instance of this policy might be recalled the celebrated case of King Juba II of Mauretania whose father Juba I had committed suicide on the occasion of Caesar's victory at Thapsus. The son, then a boy of five or six, after being carried in Caesar's triumph was brought up as a Roman citizen by Octavius (Augustus), and was eventually entrusted with the empire of the Romans in a considerable patch of north-western Africa for nearly half a century. In this spirit I like to join in thinking of a young Italianate Cogidubnus returning or being returned to his native country about the time of the Roman invasion, equipped by training as an understanding exponent of the new régime and welcomed or tolerated as a sympathetic intermediary in his own ancestral environment. The guess is at least a reasonable one.

But apart from historical inference or speculation the Fishbourne palace, whether in its splendid first-century prime or in its subsequent vicissitudes and diminutions, is full of a varied interest. Its ceremonial or administrative halls, its baths, its living-rooms, and its peripheral services are almost outrivalled by the central garden, with its frame of hedges and fences, its flower-beds and trees, and its pipes and water-basins. Nothing like it has previously been identified in so much authentic detail either in Britain or in Rome itself, in spite of ample literary and pictorial evidence for the Roman taste in these matters. No doubt future excavators, stimulated by Fishbourne, will in due course recognize intricate formal gardening as a normal feature of any sizeable Roman house. But to Professor Cunliffe will remain the credit due to the pioneer. It is to be hoped that future digging on a suitable site may discover the pollen-evidence which will complete the picture by assured re-planting. In this respect alone, Fishbourne was deficient.

And even a brief prefatory note must include an acknowledgment of the enterprising and agreeable way in which the excavated site has been roofed and displayed for the pleasurable instruction of the public. On a summer's day the crowded scene can only be described as worthy of the controlled persistence and imagination with which the excavator and his colleagues have advanced from strength to strength since that day in 1960 when 'the driver of a machine digging a trench for a water-main found that he was cutting through masses of ancient building rubble and had the good sense to mention this to the engineer in charge, who reported the discovery to the local archaeological committee ...'

MORTIMER WHEELER

Introduction

In ten years following the initial, accidental, rediscovery of the Roman palace at Fishbourne in 1960, the site has been substantially excavated, modern cover buildings have been erected, a museum built, the Roman garden laid out, and visitors now pour in at a present rate of a quarter of a million a year. Perhaps more important from the writer's point of view, the definitive excavation reports have been prepared and published.

A decade of work involving more than a thousand people, most of them volunteers, cannot be allowed to pass without some brief mention of the bodies responsible for creating the organization which made it all possible. The initial discovery was reported to a local archaeological committee and through them to the Chichester Civic Society, for Fishbourne lies within the City boundaries. Thereafter, this small Society firmly grasped the nettle, raising more than £11,000 and undertaking the entire task of organizing the domestic side of nine seasons of excavation. At an early stage the Sussex Archaeological Society took an active interest in the project and through the generosity of one of its senior members, Mr I.D. Margary, a large part of the site was purchased and vested in the Sussex Archaeological Trust. This body, with its various committees, then undertook to prepare the site for presentation to the public. Finally, when building work was well advanced, *The Sunday Times* came forward with a welcome offer to finance and organize the display of material in the site museum and to assist in the visual layout of the rest of the remains. Their professionalism has added enormously to the success of the venture.

While the organizers numbered no more than thirty, the volunteers exceeded nine hundred. It was their enthusiasm and exertions, for a total period of fifty weeks, which made the excavation possible, and with them the last word of grateful thanks must be left.

B.W.C.

Department of Archaeology
University of Southampton

I

Discovery

'There can be no doubt,' wrote the local historian Horsfield in 1835, 'that the Roman patricians and chiefs had villas in this neighbourhood, which time will some day bring to light.'[1] He was right but the day was a long way off, in fact it was not until 1960 that the first hints of a Roman palatial building began to emerge from the fields of Fishbourne.

The first recorded discoveries to which Horsfield was referring were made early in the nineteenth century when 'In digging by the roadside i.e. north and south of the main west road [now the A27] was found in 1805 a tesselated pavement about 13½ ft wide; the length was not ascertained as it ran under a hedge. In the middle of this, occupying a space about 2 feet in diameter was part of the base of a column. Immediately underneath the floor, paved with small black and white stones, was a fine spring.'[2] It seems that these discoveries were made during the construction of a house for on Friday, 18th April, 1806, at the Bull's Head, Fishbourne, the house in question was sold by auction, the notice of sale[3] stating that in addition to being 'delightfully situated ... commanding pleasing views of the Harbour and a beautiful featured inland country', it could boast a 'Curious Roman pavement 13 ft square'. The house presumably still stands over the South Wing of the Roman palace but which of the houses it is cannot now be ascertained. A few years later in 1812 'certain subterranean remains were found ... Whether they were of a hypocaust or cold bath is unknown for the discovery was imperfectly made and inaccurately reported' – James Dallaway's terse summary of the situation in his *A History of the Western Division of the County of Sussex* is fair comment on these tantalizingly elusive discoveries.

There the matter rested. A few scraps came to light later in the nineteenth century including finds of Roman pottery and tiles from the area of the watercress beds south of the village, but little attention was paid to them. Early this century, however, Fishbourne was blessed with a highly active antiquarian clergyman, the Reverend N. Shaw, who set about collecting and recording the Roman remains in his parish. From the site of his Rectory, now a housing estate, a quantity of Roman material was salvaged and was even reported in a letter to *The Times* in 1929 [4] and as late as 1936 Mr Shaw was giving advice and encouragement to a local boy who had discovered a mosaic pavement at the end of his garden, a mosaic which is known now to have belonged to the West Wing of the Roman palace. By the late 1930's, then, parts of the south and west wings of the palace had been seen, rubbish from the silt filling the Roman harbour to the south had been discovered in the watercress beds and occupation could be shown to extend along the main road towards Chichester. But no-one at this stage could believe that all these fragments belonged to a single structure.

A new impetus was given to local archaeological interests when early in 1960 a skin-diver recovered quantities of Roman building rubbish from the Mill pond south of the village, near the harbour. It was later in that year that work began on the construction of a water-main which was to run through the fields north of the village towards the Chichester by-pass and thence to Selsey. The story of the discovery, or more correctly, the rediscovery, of the Roman building in 1960 is typical of the rescue activity which is going on all over the country with increasing momentum each year as the quantity of earth-shifting construction work continues to grow, but, unlike many chance finds, because of close local co-operation the Fishbourne discovery was properly recorded and eventually followed up. The story is simple: the driver of the machine digging the trench for the water-main found that he was cutting through masses of ancient building rubble and mentioned this to the engineer in charge who examined the remains, and thinking them to be part of a tile clamp reported the find to the local archaeological committee. Two observers went out immediately to record the discovery and, much to their surprise, found not only masses of Roman roofing tiles but also walls and mosaic pavements sectioned by the trench. A rapid survey of the remains and the collection of quantities of pottery from the spoil heap was all that could be done before the trench had to be immediately refilled. But now, for the first time, the position of a large Roman building at Fishbourne was exactly known and, more important, the associated pottery showed it to belong to a very early period in the Roman occupation.

The next step was how to follow up the discovery. The Chichester Civic Society, to whom a full report was made, decided to organize an exploratory excavation of the area and the following Easter a small team of students working for three weeks cut a series of trial trenches which determined in broad outline the history of the site. [5] First there had been a series of timber buildings, then, in the late first century, the site was cleared and a very large masonry building erected, which later had undergone a series of alterations. The real shock was finding a large well-constructed masonry building of such an early date, more staggering still was that the building was floored with mosaics earlier than any previously found in England and clearly the product of immigrant craftsmen. While plans for an extended summer season of excavation were underway, it was learnt that the area was about to be offered for sale as building-land, which might well have meant the total destruction of large parts of the buried structures. It was under this threat that the first major excavation of 1961 was carried out. Excavation policy was simple: it was necessary to uncover as much of the plan of the masonry building as possible, to obtain more dating evidence for it and, even more difficult, to impress the public with the importance of the site. A series of rapid trial trenches accomplished the main aims in six weeks, the skeleton plan of more than 300 ft of building, dating to the period AD 75–80, was exposed, and seven mosaics were uncovered. One of these, the dolphin mosaic, found on the last afternoon of the excavation, symbolized the whole atmosphere of the first year: it was discovered in a narrow trial trench, pushed westwards into an unknown area, just wide enough to show the head of a centrally placed cupid with sea beasts on either side of him, one emerging from the unexcavated soil, the other disappearing into it. From a public relations point of view there could hardly have been a more dramatic ending to the season.

Throughout the next year negotiations for the purchase of the land on behalf of the Sussex Archaeological Trust advanced well and by the summer of 1962, when the second season's work began, the future of the site seemed assured. Work could therefore be concentrated on the large-scale area excavation of the archaeologically important, but less spectacular, timber buildings which lay beneath the East Wing of the masonry building. Gradually it became possible to untangle the early history of the site, before the great Roman building was erected in the late first century obscuring everything.

In the following years the excavations took in new areas. In 1963 the North Wing from the dolphin mosaic westwards was uncovered, together with part of the newly discovered West Wing and during the next season most of the remainder of the North and West Wings were exposed In 1965 work concentrated on the audience chamber in the West Wing and the great entrance hall opposite in the East Wing, but now for the first time it was realized that the central courtyard, more than 250 ft across, had been laid out as a great formal garden in the Roman period, the excavation of which was to last for two more years.

Until 1966 work had been largely concerned with that part of the Roman site which lay to the north of the main road on land belonging to the Sussex Archaeological Trust, but some limited trenching in the gardens of the houses south of the road, the general area of the 1805 finds, gradually led to the recovery of the plan of the bath suite which lay at the south end of the East Wing. Until this time, however, there was little evidence as to how the south side of the garden was treated: there were innumerable possibilities but no positive evidence. The problem was finally resolved in 1967 when the owner of one of the houses in the crucial area invited us to excavate in his garden. Within a very short time it was possible to trace the main lines of a hitherto unsuspected South Wing 300 ft long and 70 ft wide, closing the great courtyard on its southern side. Although very little further excavation could be carried out here because the main road covered most of the wing, it seemed at last that the principal limits of the palace had been reached. But this was not so. At Easter 1969, in response to the development of a housing estate over the rather marshy area south of the South Wing, a close watch was kept on the foundation trenches which were cut for the buildings and a number of exploratory trenches were dug for archaeological reasons. The results were indisputable. Instead of the palace ending on its South Wing, the Roman built-up area continued further south across another vast garden to the sea some 350 ft away, and in the mud and silt filling of the artificially created lagoon beyond were found quantities of leather and wooden objects in an excellent state of preservation. At the present moment it is intended to carry out further excavations in what promises to be one of the most interesting parts of the entire Roman complex.

The excavation of Fishbourne, in its later stages, ran parallel with the construction of protective buildings, a museum and the other facilities which were erected by the Sussex Archaeological Trust, so that the site could be put on permanent display to the public. The construction was not without its problems but at an early stage it was decided not to attempt any close reconstruction of the Roman superstructure. Instead a cover building of timber, glass and aluminium designed in a blatantly non-Roman style was erected exactly upon the footings of the North Wing of the Roman palace, an area containing the more visually attractive exhibits. The aim of the building was two-fold: to create a protective environment over the delicate Roman structures and to offer some idea of the mass, if not the detail, of the original Roman building when viewed from the outside.

After the cover building had been completed and the protective covering of soil removed from the Roman floors for the last time, work began on the complex process involved in consolidating and conserving the ancient features. Temperature and humidity control had to be finely adjusted to prevent the growth of algae and fungi, walls needed impregnation and those mosaics which had become loosened by centuries of root growth and worm action were carefully lifted and relaid. No attempt was made to repair holes or breaks in the patterned mosaics, but the red tesselated floors were reconstructed where areas were missing. This posed problems because it was necessary to show a difference between the original work and the patches, but the answer was found by setting the newly-laid tesserae in a waterproof cement so that they always appear drier than the originals. Another problem arose when the supply of loose Roman tesserae ran out but new ones were quickly made by a mosaicist from Roman tiles and bricks, and to remove their fresh appearance they were tumbled together for a while in a cement mixer.

Gradually obstacles like these were overcome and the building took shape, while the garden was replanted along its original Roman lines. Finally the museum was completed and its interior arrangement carefully designed to use the objects found during the excavations, together with other graphic material, to tell the story of the site from the time of its first occupation in the Mesolithic period until the excavation began in 1961.

II

Inhabitants and Invaders

The upper reaches of the Chichester Inlet had for a long time been attractive to man, for they provided safe anchorage, a plentiful supply of fish and wildfowl and gently shelving beaches suitable for the extraction of salt. The earliest trace of human activity at Fishbourne came in the form of two flint axes, known as tranchet axes because of the cross blow used to remove sharpening flakes. These implements, a general-purpose heavy tool, belong to the Mesolithic period, well back in the fifth or fourth millennium BC. One was found in the deep silt which began to clog the inlet following the end of the Ice Age when, as the result of melting ice, the sea-level began to rise. Presumably the harbour end was frequented by Mesolithic hunters in search of food, it may even be that a temporary settlement of the period lies somewhere nearby, but no trace of it has yet been found.

The need of primitive societies for salt is clearly reflected in the archaeology of the harbours of the Solent where traces of evaporation pans, clay supports and flues connected with the Iron Age salt extraction are frequently found. At Fishbourne a few fragments of this briquetage have been recorded from an early beach level but so far no trace of extensive activity is known. On the dry land nearby, however, pottery of the first century BC has turned up in the excavation in small quantities which suggests the use of the harbour area by late Iron Age communities, but whether because of its sea communications, salt-producing facilities or simply its fertile hinterland, cannot be said.

For fifty years or so before Caesar's invasions of Britain in 55 and 54 BC the societies of south and east Britain were undergoing widespread change, partly as the result of an influx of new peoples arriving from the turmoil on the adjacent continent and partly because of internal conflict. Innovations introduced during this period include a coin economy, the use of the wheel for turning pottery, rotary querns for grinding corn and no doubt many other improvements more difficult to define. One development of some significance, which appeared at this time in parts of south-eastern Britain, was the use of massively-constructed linear earth-

works, dividing off large tracts of land, for defence. Often these earthworks would run from one river valley to another, sometimes they would
end apparently without reason. A splendid series of earthworks of this
class divide up the coastal plain for miles around Chichester, running east-
west across the gravel plain from one river valley to the next and north-
south from the edge of the chalk downs to the sea. A recent study of these
Chichester Entrenchments[6] and of a similar series around the Belgic
capital of Camulodunum in Essex has shown that they belong to the last
stages of the pre-Roman Iron Age. They appear to be the ultimate in pre-
Roman defensive architecture built to defend not only a community but
perhaps several communities together with their fields, livestock and
grazing land. It has been suggested that the earthworks were designed
primarily against the chariot war-fare which had been developed to a
fine art by this time. For this reason they stopped on the thickly wooded
valleys and on other woods through which vehicles could not pass. This
theory has its attractions and may well be close to the truth.

The Chichester Entrenchments were evidently designed to protect not
only the hinterland around the site of the later town of Chichester, but
also the harbours of the Fishbourne region and the whole of the Selsey
peninsula to the south, which aerial photography has shown w as covered
with acres of early field systems. It is tempting to see the light brickearth
soils of the peninsula as the principal arable land, while the clayey gravels
further north were left to scrub and woodland to provide grazing and
pannage for the flocks and herds. Within this territory would presumably
have been the main urban or semi-urban centre of the region which in all
probability lay in the area south of the present position of Selsey Bill. It
is well known that massive coastal erosion has swept away many square
miles of land even in historical times. In all probability the pre-Roman
settlement has long since disappeared into the sea. All that has remained
is a wide selection of gold coins washed up from time to time on the
shore. Selsey was not the only settlement within the defended territory:
two others, possibly individual farms, are known, one north and the other
east of present-day Chichester and there are probably many others. But
there is no evidence at all to suggest that a settlement of this date grew
up on the site of Chichester itself.

The political situation in Britain in the century before the invasion of
AD 43 was, to say the least, complex.[7] Ruling households rose to power
from which individual kings would emerge to govern for a time before
dying or being deposed. Sometimes they followed pro-Roman policies,

Fig. 1

at other times they were anti-Roman. This, and no doubt other causes, led to constant warring between tribes and also, apparently, quarrelling within the tribes, but how far these dynastic events affected the average peasant farmer is very difficult to assess. Life for the bulk of the population probably continued much as before no matter which political party was in power.

The general trend in policies and allegiances can be tolerably well pieced together using the evidence provided by changing types of coins, together with the casual documentary references to the British scene found in the contemporary classical sources. The first ruler of central southern Britain whose name survives is Commius, first a friend and later an avowed enemy of Caesar, who narrowly escaped assassination by fleeing to Britain from Gaul, apparently to join his people who had already settled here. The distribution of his coins suggests control over the area stretching from the middle Thames valley south into Hampshire and West Sussex, the territory belonging to the tribe known as the Atrebates.

Commius ruled until about 20 BC when he was succeeded by his son Tincommius. At first Tincommius issued coins of traditional form, each depicting a triple-tailed horse, but some time soon after 16 BC the design changed and a totally new type was introduced, copying a Roman denarius minted by the Emperor Augustus between 15 and 12 BC. These coins are so close to the original Roman model that a Roman engraver must have been employed to cut the die. This change, though superficially simple, may well have marked a complete turnabout in policy from the strong anti-Roman tradition of Commius to a new pro-Roman attitude. Some supporting evidence is provided by contemporary Roman writers: in 27 BC Dio tells us that the Britons would not come to terms with Rome, whereas Horace, in an ode published in 13 BC, refers to Caesar's suppliants in Britain. Presumably, therefore, the tough anti-Roman line of some at least of the British rulers had softened during this period: in all probability Tincommius was one.

But such a *volte-face* could not have been easy for the older members of the Atrebatic aristocracy to accept. Coin evidence again suggests that the Dobunni, one time allies of the Atrebates, living in Gloucestershire and Somerset, would have none of it and broke away, subsequently to join with the powerful Catuvellauni. Internally, too, there seems to have been trouble, for by AD 7 Tincommius had fled to the Emperor in Rome to ask for help. Tincommius did not return, but instead was replaced by his brother Epillus who styled himself *Rex* on his coins, implying perhaps some form of imperial recognition from Rome. But his rule over the Atrebates was short and although he appears to have continued to issue coins in Kent, the old kingdom seems by now to have been taken over by the third brother, Verica.

1 The Fishbourne-Chichester region

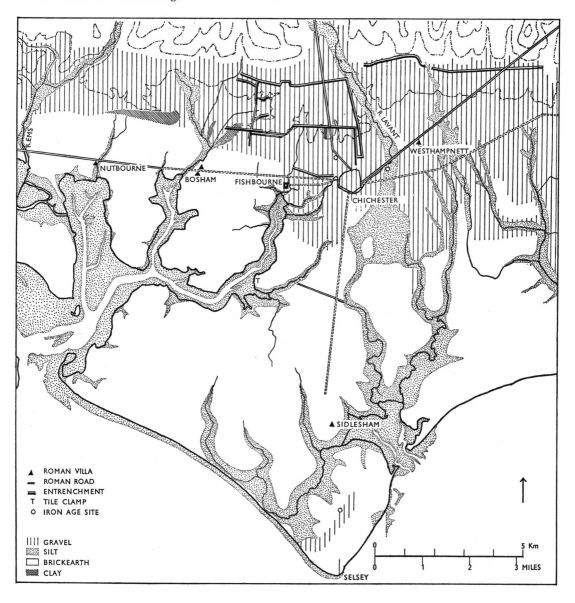

If the coin evidence is reliable, Verica maintained close connections with Roman culture, continuing to use the title *Rex* and copying coins of Tiberius. He even at one stage introduced the vine-leaf emblem to demonstrate, some suggest, his preference for Roman wine. All the time imported Roman goods continued to reach the kingdom through ports such as Hengistbury Head near Christchurch, and probably Selsey.

In other parts of Britain policies were different. In the Thames valley and eastern Britain were the hostile warlike Catuvellauni, who were later to lead military opposition against the Roman armies. By AD 25 the Catuvellauni were expanding south into Atrebatic territory, Epaticus, one of their leaders, soon gaining control of the northern Atrebatic capital of Calleva (later the Roman town of Silchester). Coin distribution suggests that Catuvellaunian aggression from the north continued to carve deeply into the old Atrebatic kingdom, until by the early 40's of the first century AD Verica's kingdom was reduced to a small corner of south-east Hampshire and south-west Sussex, centred upon the Chichester-Selsey region. This view is to some extent supported by the archaeological evidence, which suggests that while the old style hill forts in Verica's reduced kingdom remained derelict, those in the anti-Roman areas, in east Sussex, the Weald and the chalk uplands west of the Test, were put in defensive order, probably against the threat of Roman attack.

The end of Verica's rule came in about AD 42, when at last the old king was forced to flee the country and run to the Emperor Claudius for support. Superficially it might appear that external military factors finally dislodged him, but it may be that dissident elements within the Atrebates were responsible – we are unlikely ever to know. At any event, the general political situation in 42–3 is clear enough: the Chichester region with its superb harbours was still largely pro-Roman in attitude and more-over, since it was now under pressure from its enemies, it had come to rely heavily upon Roman support. To the north, in eastern Britain, the Thames valley and spreading into Wiltshire, were the hostile Catuvellauni, now closely aligned with the Dobunni further west in Gloucestershire; west of the River Test and extending across Dorset into Devon and Somerset, was another violently anti-Roman tribe, the Durotriges, who had developed from a deep rooted native stock virtually untouched by the folk movements of the first century BC. Thus, in a broad arc from Kent to Dorset, lived those opposed to Rome and her policies. The situation in east Kent and east Sussex is less clear, but again the general appearance is of opposition. With his diminishing kingdom hedged in by enemies on three sides and the sea on the fourth, it is hardly surprising that the ageing Verica looked to Rome, the traditional ally of his people, for help.

On the Roman side, Verica's flight was opportune. Britain had always been shrouded with an air of mystery, there were rumours of great mineral wealth but more important it served as a haven for dissidents who could conveniently sail across to Gaul to cause trouble for the Roman government. For these reasons, and no doubt for personal glorification, Caesar had led two military expeditions into the country in 55 and again in 54 BC. Even his own accounts of the events hardly cover up the near-disasters which he experienced, but, while in a military sense the expeditions failed, politically he could claim to have supported friendly tribes against aggressors and extracted a promise of annual tribute. He may well have intended to return again to carry out a more thorough job but pressing problems arose to require his presence elsewhere. The Britons were left to themselves and soon the tribute to Rome ceased to be paid. Augustus was uneasy about the British situation: it was an irritant but of minor importance compared with some of his problems, and so long as diplomatic relations could be kept going he was content to leave things much as they were. By the time Gaius had come to power, Britain had taken on a new importance. Massive military preparations were put in hand at Boulogne, a fleet was built and the harbour remodelled. But all this came to nothing when the recalcitrant army was ineptly led to the sea-shore by Gaius and made to pick up sea-shells as a mark of his contempt for their mutinous fear of Britain. Nevertheless the fleet and the naval installations remained.

When, in AD 41, Claudius rather unexpectedly became emperor, he began to consider Britain with growing interest. To consolidate his rather shaky position he needed a military triumph in Rome, but to become eligible for so high an honour it was necessary to annex a new territory for Rome with a minimum loss of Roman life. Britain was the obvious area, it was relatively near at hand and suitable preparations had, after all, been made by Gaius. Pride came into this too: Britain was always something of an embarrassment to Rome after Caesar had established an interest in the island. The Britons would not come to terms; such arrogance could hardly be allowed to remain so close to the empire.

The arrival of Verica in Rome must have been a deciding factor, the ruler of one of Rome's oldest British allies was asking for help. A British campaign could now be presented in terms of Rome's support for her friends in their time of need. More important, Verica must have brought with him an intimate knowledge not only of the country but of the detailed political situation. Such intelligence information would have been essential for the planning of a successful operation.

In AD 43, after an inauspicious beginning during which the troops, fearful of the sea and what lay beyond, at first refused to budge, the invasion force set sail from Boulogne under the command of Aulus Plautius. It was split into three arms, says the historian Cassius Dio, so that a unified landing would not be opposed. [8] This statement, and the fact that Dio says that after some trouble ships were guided west by a comet, has led some archaeologists to suggest that the invasion force was divided into three equal prongs aimed at widely spaced beach-heads around the south-east shores of Britain. The problem cannot easily be resolved but it is most unlikely that Plautius would have fragmented his force to any great extent, since consolidated strength was needed above all in the initial stages. The excavations at Richborough in Kent, [9] have shown beyond doubt that a very considerable force landed here in 43, suggesting that the promontory formed the initial base at which the troops were reformed into their fighting units. Very soon beach-head fortifications consisting of a double ditch backed by a rampart were thrown up to protect stores and unloading procedures. From here the first thrust was made through Kent to the Medway where the massed armies of the British tribes, led by the Catuvellaunian rulers Togodubnus and Caratacus, were waiting. After a bitter two-day battle, at which Vespasian, the young legate in charge of the second legion, distinguished himself, the resistance was smashed, Togodubnus was killed and Caratacus was forced to flee. The Roman advance to the Thames and the crossing of the river were largely unopposed. Here Plautius rested, waiting for the Emperor Claudius to join him and lead the final thrust deep into the territory of the Catuvellauni, culminating in the destruction of the Catuvellaunian capital of Camulodunum. The task accomplished, Claudius retired home again to enjoy his much desired triumph.

The initial advance had been fast, well-timed and an unqualified success, but no commander would have dared to make such a deep inroad into enemy territory without first assuring the safety of his flanks. For Plautius geography helped. His route to the Thames along the North Downs was well protected on one side by the sea and on the other, to some extent, by the Wealden forest. But the Weald was not as impenetrable as was once supposed. Potentially it might have formed a dangerous rallying ground for tribal armies coming in from the south-west to join the anti-Roman cause. What may well have prevented this was the presence of Verica's Atrebates conveniently placed between the Durotriges and the area of initial Roman advance. The significance of their position cannot have failed to have impressed the Roman military planners. While there is absolutely no positive proof, it would seem probable that some small force was landed in the territory at the beginning of the invasion to provide physical or moral support for the pro-Roman faction and to ensure that the area remained friendly while the first rapid troop movements were being carried out in Kent. This might well be one of the three landing parties implied in the account of Dio. Moreover the Chichester area is conveniently west of Boulogne – the direction in which the comet helped to guide some ships.

The political stabilization of the Atrebatic kingdom was important to the early consolidation of the province, particularly as an example to neighbouring tribes of how the Romans treated their friends and allies. First the occupying authorities would have needed a figure-head at the same time acceptable to the natives and managable by Rome. Verica, the obvious choice, does not seem to have been brought back; several reasons may account for this: as a son of Commius he must by 43 have been a very old man, if indeed he was still alive, but, more important, it may have been internal troubles that forced him to run to Rome; to return such a man would have been dangerous. The person singled out to replace him was Tiberius Claudius Cogidubnus, a shadowy but intensely interesting personality who dominated the Chichester region for more than thirty years after the invasion, and with whose fortunes it is believed the early history of Fishbourne was closely bound.

Our slight factual knowledge of Cogidubnus comes from two sources. The Roman historian Tacitus, writing of him, says that 'he maintained his unswerving loyalty to our own times' and that certain cantons (estates) were given to him.[10] The second source is a remarkable inscription carved on Purbeck marble, which was dug up near the centre of Chichester in 1723.[11] It records the erection of a Temple of Neptune and Minerva to the honour of the Divine Household, that is the household of the emperor, by a guild of craftsmen. It was erected with the authority of Tiberius Claudius Cogidubnus, who is given the title of *Rex, legatus augusti in Britannia* – 'king and legate to the emperor in Britain'. Together these two sources show that Cogidubnus was a client king responsible for the area in which Chichester is situated. His name, incorporating the Celtic

Plate 2

dubno or *dumno* meaning powerful or deep, clearly implies that he was a native but had been granted Roman citizenship under Claudius, whose first names he adopted. The people living in the Chichester region soon became known as the *Regnenses* ('the people of the kingdom') and the new Roman town which grew up at Chichester was called *Noviomagus Regnensium* ('the new market [or clearing] of the people of the kingdom'), implying that the town replaced an old centre which may have been at Selsey. The kingdom, then, over which Cogidubnus ruled was the old Atrebatic territory to which additional areas were added. The second part of Cogidubnus' remarkable title, *legatus augusti,* will be considered again later, since there is some reason to believe that it was not awarded for some time after the invasion.

That Cogidubnus succeeded Verica is clear, but when and why? Unfortunately there can be no firm answers. One possibility is that he was a member of the ruling household, next in succession to Verica, who took over when the old man fled or perhaps he even ousted him. Alternatively, he may simply have been a promising young man picked out by the Romans as a potential leader when they landed, and set up to run the kingdom for them. There are, however, two things that can be said of him: he was successful and he seems to have enthusiastically embraced Roman culture from an early date (this much will appear in following chapters). It is likely therefore that he was a member of the ruling household able to command respect and support, and that he was well versed in the Roman way of life.

Now, it was a general policy of the early emperors to encourage young men of noble families from the barbarian fringes to live in Rome, either as refugees from their homeland or as hostages, so that they could be inculcated with Roman culture and values. The return of such a policy for the Romans is self-evident: it appealed tremendously to Claudius, always the shrewd manipulator. One instance of its practical value is well documented:[12] the Cherusci, a German tribe who lived north of the Rhine frontier, emerged from a period of bitter civil war, having slaughtered their aristocracy. The only surviving member of the nobility was a young prince, Italicus, nephew of the famous German war-lord Arminius. His mother had been held hostage and he had been born and reared in Rome, virtually as a Roman. When the Cherusci appealed to Claudius to send them a leader, Claudius selected Italicus, reminding him that he was the first man born in Rome as a Roman citizen to rule a foreign throne. It is tempting to see in the life and aspirations of Cogidubnus a similar Roman training. Perhaps he, too, had been taken to Rome as a child and educated there, to be returned to his homeland and people on the eve of the Roman conquest. We will never know, but this is part of the attraction which the character of the man holds for us.

Speculation apart, it can be said that Cogidubnus was installed as a client king at the beginning of the invasion period. Apart from maintaining the pro-Roman policies of his kingdom, his main function in the first weeks would have been to create a stable buffer on the left flank of the advancing army and its supply lines. At the same time, by demonstrating the benefits of his allegiance with Rome, he would probably have attempted to win over neighbouring rulers, persuading them to offer their submission to the advancing legions. The Dobunni, whose capitulation is recorded in Dio's narrative while the army were still crossing Kent, may well have submitted direct to Cogidubnus; there were probably others, too, who were ready to throw in their lot with the invaders.

Was he, as some writers have said, a quisling or was he a man of vision tired of petty tribal squabbles who saw in Rome the possibility of a peace and cultural advance never before experienced by Britain?

III

The Military Occupation

Plate 1
Fig. 2

The earliest buildings to be defined at Fishbourne belong to the period immediately following the invasion of AD 43; in form they suggest close connections with the military authorities. The attraction of the site clearly lay in the close proximity of a good harbour set in a well-protected position at the head of a wide inlet. Originally the navigable waters would have been T-shaped in plan with a main north-south channel leading to two lateral channels set at right-angles to it. Of these only the eastern channel has been partly examined by excavation: the western channel has been somewhat obscured by the construction of a large mill-pond which now fills much of its valley. Although excavation of this eastern inlet has only just begun and much remains to be discovered, we now know that the shallow gravel-floored valley was cut by several channels kept free from silt by two fresh-water streams flowing in from the north and east. One at least of the channels had been artificially widened and deepened and its sides lined with dry-walling of large stone blocks. Treatment of this kind would have allowed barges to reach within two hundred feet of the buildings. Some hints are now beginning to emerge of even more elaborate harbour works nearer the mouth of the main channel, where a spur of dry land pushed down between the inlets. Further to the south in the main channel there would have been unlimited deep-water anchorage for larger ships, well protected from storms and violent seas by twists and turns in the lower reaches of the creek. Such were the physical advantages of Fishbourne harbour.

The main site to be excavated lay at the head of the eastern inlet. Here the clayey gravel sub-soil sloped down gently to a gravel-floored valley, through which flowed a small stream barely 10 ft across. The site as we now know it was divided into three strips by two parallel roads built of rammed gravel, both of which crossed the stream by means of fords. Excavations beneath the roads showed that they had been laid directly on the untouched soil before any signs of occupation rubbish had been allowed to accumulate. Two buildings of this early period were found and completely excavated, one lying between the roads, the other to the north of the northern road. Part of a third building was seen in a trial trench dug south of the southern road.

The first building, an elongated structure more than 100 ft long and 24 ft wide, lay on a north-south axis between the two roads. As the ground-plan shows, it was a complex structure based on a series of vertical timbers 6–9 ins in diameter, which had been set in six parallel trenches dug 2 ft deep into the natural gravel. The verticals were kept in position by the spoil which had been tightly packed back into the trenches. Later, after the timbers had rotted, darker soil from above fell into the

Plate 5

Fig. 3

2   *The upper reaches of Chichester Harbour. The position of the Flavian Palace is shown by the broken line*

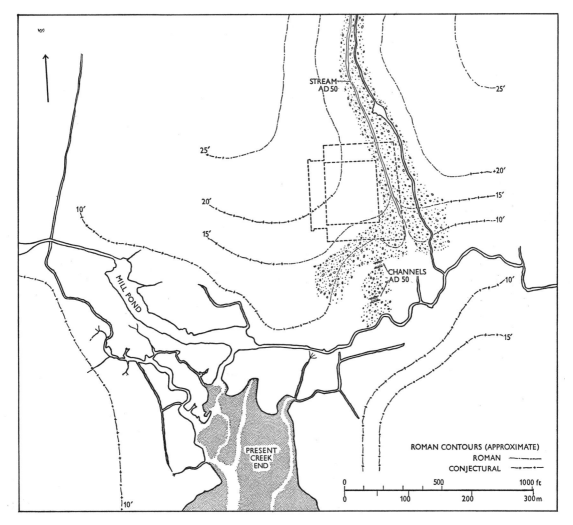

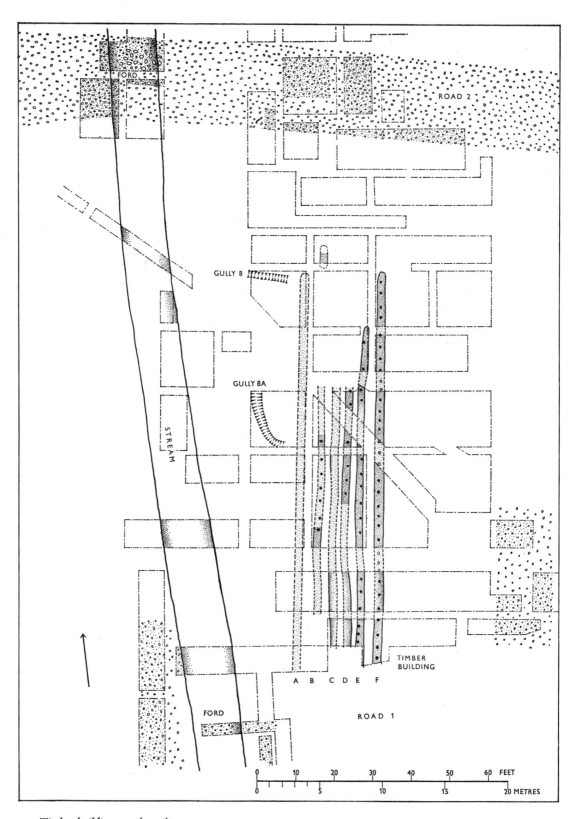

ROAD 2

GULLY 8

GULLY 8A

STREAM

TIMBER
BUILDING

A B C D E F

FORD

FORD

ROAD 1

| 0 | 10 | 20 | 30 | 40 | 50 | 60 FEET |

| 0 | 5 | 10 | 15 | 20 METRES |

3   *Timber building 1 – the military granary*

voids. Therefore when the excavation had reached the appropriate level it was possible to recognize three types of soil texture and colour: the tightly-packed undisturbed natural gravel, the looser gravelly soil packed back into the trenches and a much darker soil filling the old post-holes. On this basis, although the building had completely disappeared, its plan was recoverable by excavation.

Since the vertical timbers were spaced closely together, on a grid about 3 ft apart, they could not have stood to the full height of the building. It is almost certain, therefore, that they were no more than piles projecting 2 or 3 ft above the soil to take a platform of joists, upon which the rest of the building was erected. Raised floors of this kind are a well-known feature of the Roman military buildings used as granaries, the floor serving two functions: to keep the corn above the damp ground and well ventilated, and to prevent the easy approach of destructive rodents. Exactly how the superstructure was designed cannot now be discovered, but all that was required was some simple form of single-storied erection with walls strong enough to take the thrust of grain piled up against them. Judging by the amount of tile fragments lying around, the roof was tiled, no doubt to reduce the risk of fire. The north end of the building was more simply constructed than the rest, without the close-spaced rows of piles. The explanation for this would seem to be that the area formed part of a covered loading bay, and that the raised

Fig. 4

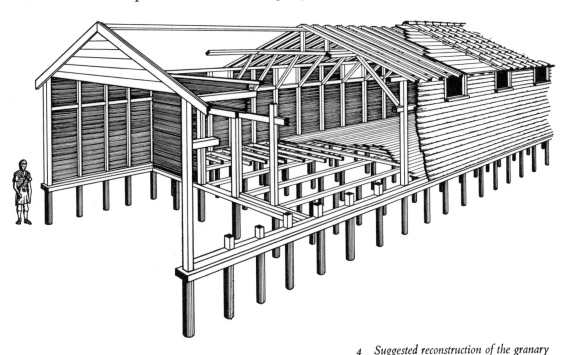

4   *Suggested reconstruction of the granary*

timber floor here would not need to be as massively supported as that of the southern part of the building, where the deadweight of the stores lay.

The structure of the building implies that it served the specialized function of a granary. Granaries of this general type are well-known on Roman military sites, usually built in masonry, but in Britain more than twelve similar timber structures were found at the great military supply base at Richborough, a depot which superseded the initial bridgehead fortification mentioned above. Here they evidently housed a vast reserve stock capable of feeding many thousands of troops. Another close parallel was provided by a similarly constructed, though much larger, building found in the supply depot at Rödgen, near Bad Nauheim in Germany,[13] built some years earlier than Fishbourne and Richborough. Clearly the basic structural principles involved in timber granary construction were well established and widely used in military practice.

Fig. 5
Plates 6, 7

The second timber building fronted onto the northern road. Again it was constructed of timbers but this time they were set individually in post pits about 3 ft in diameter and of equivalent depth, set at a spacing of about eight or nine foot intervals, forming a building about 100 ft by 50 ft. Exactly how the superstructure was designed cannot now be reconstructed, but here again the posts probably supported a raised timber floor since no trace of a floor level or of any form of wear could be found on the surface of the original soil beneath. It may be that the vertical timbers continued to the full height of the building so that they could be used as a basis for internal partitions. An arrangement of this kind would have been useful if the interior was divided up into bins for loose grain. The rows of timbers on the north and south sides of the building were less regularly spaced than the others, possibly because they formed some kind of veranda or covered loading platform. The northern road was laid right up to the south front and was much wider here than further east, probably to create a well metalled apron so that carts could easily turn round, pass each other or back up to the unloading area. The north side of the building was also flanked by a gravelled area 15 ft wide, which had been provided with shallow side ditches to facilitate drainage. This tends to support the idea of a veranda along the north side, but it can never have been used for major loading and unloading like the south front.

Parallels to the building, though by no means common, can be found in other military contexts. The little fort built into the corner of the Iron Age hill fort at Hod Hill in Dorset[14] has a granary constructed in an almost identical fashion but with the posts a little more closely spaced, and

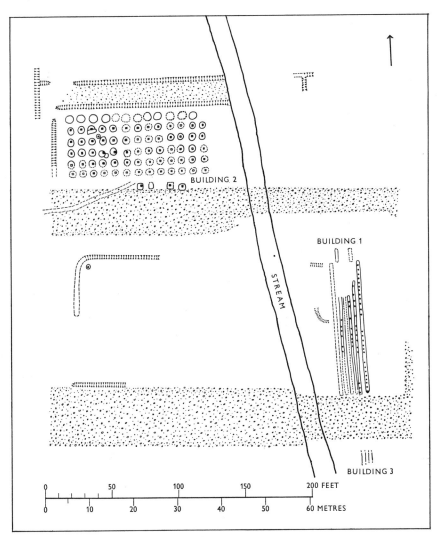

5 The arrangement of the Claudian military buildings

in Germany, at the supply base of Rödgen, several buildings, probably
for storage, have been found which are closely similar in plan to the Fishbourne structure. Both buildings, then, can be seen to have counterparts
in well attested military contexts, leaving little doubt that the Fishbourne
structures were erected under military control.

What has been described so far can only be a small part of a very much
larger settlement, of which only a few other details are known. South of
building 1 a fragment of the plan of an almost identical structure was

uncovered in a trial trench dug in a private garden, while south of building 2, between the two roads, a ditched enclosure was found which could have been used as a kraal for livestock. Cattle in particular would have formed an essential part of military supplies, providing not only meat but also the hides and lard so essential for an army on the march.

The date at which the buildings were erected cannot be given with absolute precision, for the archaeological material does not allow close dating. Nevertheless the base was laid out on a site which had not been previously occupied, and from the earliest occupation layers associated with them come quantities of coins and pottery of the types in use at the very beginning of the Roman occupation of Britain. Some of the pottery, in particular certain of the samian ware (pottery with a distinctive glossy red fabric manufactured in Gaul) is found on continental sites dating to the late 30's and early 40's of the first century AD. It would not normally be expected to occur in this country much after 45.

The coins also point to early military beginnings. Two main types are found: the small silver denarii used to pay the soldiers, often old worn coins still in use after 40 or 50 years of service, and the larger bronze issues (ases) of Claudius, of which more than 60 have been found in the early levels at Fishbourne. Most of these are copies, of varying quality, struck in this country, probably under contract to the army to overcome a shortage of small change. The Claudian copies occur in large numbers on early military sites but continue to be used well into the Neronian period.

Beside the pottery, coins and other trinkets commonly found on Roman sites, both civil and military, several objects of military equipment have been recovered. These include a decorated belt-plate, belt buckles and several small strap buckles and strap hinges from military uniforms. The only weapon of distinctly military type to be found is the head of an iron ballista bolt exactly like those known to have been fired by the Roman army in great volleys at the native defenders of the hill forts of Hod Hill and Maiden Castle. But perhaps the most interesting piece of military equipment from Fishbourne is a bronze legionary's helmet which was dredged up from the harbour in the nineteenth century, and is now in the British Museum. The helmet is well preserved and still retains its wide neck-flap to protect the neck from sword slashes and the visor above the forehead to deflect glancing blows from the face. It is tempting to think of it as being dropped overboard by a legionary about to disembark.

Fig. 6

Plate 3

1 Fishbourne from the air, looking north, at low tide. The position of the two east-west creek ends shows up as low-lying waterlogged land. The palace lay astride the present main road, in the centre of the picture

EPIVNOFTMINFIV
TEMPLVM
SALVEEDO   DIVINAI
AVGTORIEA   LAD
IDVBNIR   GNBR
GIVMFABRORE   INT
D S D DONANTEADAM
ENTE PVDENTINE FII

2 The Cogidubnus inscription was unearthed in Chichester in 1723 and is now displayed on the wall of the Assembly Rooms. It records the erection of a temple to Neptune and Minerva by a guild of craftsmen, by permission of Tiberius Claudius Cogidubnus, king and legate to the Emperor

3 A Roman legionary helmet dredged up in Chichester harbour, not far from Fishbourne. An oyster shell, still in position, was found attached to its crest

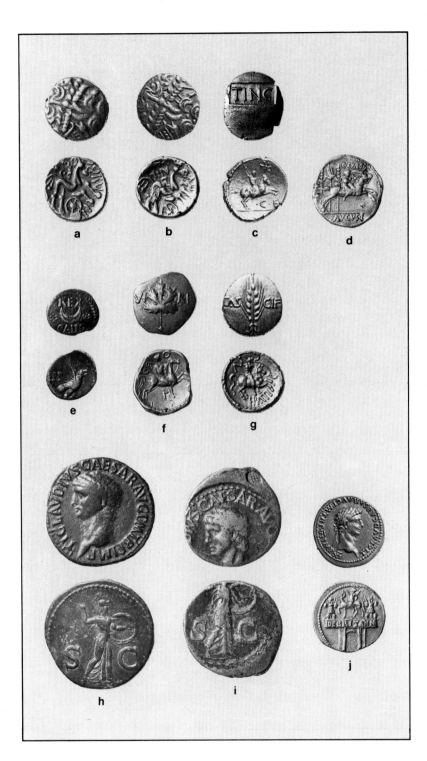

4 Examples of some of the coins current before and during the early occupation of the palace at Fishbourne. *a–c*, *e* and *f*, are Ancient British gold staters of, *a*. Commius; *b*. Tincommius, type I; *c*. Tincommius, type II; *d*. the reverse of a Roman silver denarius of Augustus, possibly the prototype for the reverse of *c*; *e*. a silver quarter-stater of Eppillus; *f*. Verica; *g*. Epaticcus; *h*. an official Roman issue of the bronze *as* of Claudius compared with, *i*, one of the local British, unofficial, copies; *j*. the gold aureus of Claudius commemorating, on its reverse type, the conquest of Britain with a triumphal arch and the legend DE BRITANN. (All coins actual size)

5 The military granary, during excavation, was represented only by the soil-filled holes where the posts had once stood. The posts had originally been set in continuous foundation trenches, which can still be made out in contrast to the undisturbed natural subsoil. The footings and the walls belong to the Flavian palace

6 One of the posts of the store building half sectioned during excavation. The circular outline of the original post-pit can be seen. The post, about 12 ins in diameter, stood in the centre where the void now is. It had been kept in position by the gravel filling of the pit

7   General view across the military store building north of the northern road. The structure of the building was supported by a grid of posts placed at 8 ft intervals. The positions for six of them can be seen, the post in the bottom left had been cut into by a later demolition pit but its void is visible, the others had all been dug out when the building fell into disrepair

8 The bridge by which the northern road crossed the stream. The western abutment, shown here, was constructed of a row of revetting posts, taking the main span of the bridge with a causeway of rubble and gravel leading out to it

9 The culvert, running across the area later occupied by the West Wing of the palace, cut through the walls of a Neronian building. Nothing is known of its ultimate destination or exact function

10 A general view across the > North Wing of the palace, looking south. In the near trench a drainage gully of the first period can be seen, partly excavated. Its course beneath the building is marked by the subsidence of the later floors into its partly consolidated filling

11 Opus sectile elements. Quantities of these shapes of coloured stone were found in levels contemporary with the Neronian proto-palace. They would have been used largely for floor decoration. The elements here are arranged in patterns, based on those found at Pompeii and Herculaneum

12 From the builders' working yard contemporary with the construction of the proto-palace came quantities of waste material, showing the various ways in which the masons worked the stone. The fragments illustrated were scored by multiple-bladed saws

13 An ornate Corinthian capital reconstructed from fragments found re-used as packing stones for posts in the Flavian garden. The columns were probably once incorporated in the garden or building of the proto-palace. The style is unusually elaborate for such an early period

14 Part of a Corinthian capital in a somewhat simple style. The original location of these columns is unknown

15, 16   Two of the mosaics from the West Wing of the Flavian palace (Plate 15 is in room
W6, Plate 16 in W3). Both are characteristic of the late first century floors at Fishbourne:
they are black and white and arranged in plain geometric patterns. The floors of the West
Wing have suffered considerably from ploughing and robbing. The strip across Plate 16 survived only because a later wall had once been mortared to it. Part of the wall, of third-period
date, remains in position, bottom left

17–19   Two of the Flavian mosaics in the West Wing (17 in room W7, 19 in corridor W13) with a detail, *below*, of the border of Plate 17, which depicts a stylized tendril drawn largely in black but with the nodes infilled alternately with red and yellow. *Opposite*, is the plain floor of a corridor; the centre had worn out and had been patched with areas of pink mortar

20 Part of the West Wing seen from the apse of the audience chamber, looking north. Very little of the superstructure of the walls has survived the robbing and ploughing to which the area was subjected in Saxon and Medieval times

21 Part of the West Wing, looking south towards the audience chamber. In the foreground is a small heated room, the floor of which had once been supported on a pillared hypocaust. The stoking chamber lay in the room beyond

22   The audience chamber in the centre of the West Wing. The apsidal recess can be clearly seen; it had once been lined by a timber bench. The mosaic floor has almost entirely disappeared, except for a small patch in the corner. The proximity of modern gardens unfortunately prevents further excavation

There is, then, reasonable evidence for a military supply base at the head of Fishbourne harbour at the beginning of the Roman invasion in AD 43, but before considering the wider implications of this it is necessary to say something of the nature of the base and its relationship to Chichester. The excavation has demonstrated the existence of several store buildings together with facilities for barges to unload or load nearby. The remains, as we know them at present, are clearly part of a specialized installation and not a fort or camp of normal type. More buildings may well come to light when it becomes possible to extend the excavation further to the east, but until the limits of the base have been defined there is little to be gained by discussing such problems as storage capacity and detailed function. Nevertheless the general impression gained is that we are looking essentially at the warehouses of a military harbour and that the camp or temporary fort lies elsewhere on a site chosen more for its military potentialities. The obvious candidate is Chichester itself. While it is true that no incontrovertible evidence of military occupation has yet come to light, excavations are gradually amassing an impressive array of very early occupation levels and recently a substantial early ditch which could be military has been found beneath the later cremation cemetery which grew up outside the Eastgate of the later Roman city. Add to this a number of pieces of bronze military equipment, recovered mainly from the eastern part of the walled area, and the evidence for military occupation begins to look impressive. No doubt further excavations will gradually modify and extend the picture, but we may tentatively assume that the main centre of military occupation lay somewhere beneath the town with Fishbourne as its harbour settlement, a mile away.

Arrangements of this kind are known elsewhere in the country. In Essex the fortress for the twentieth legion was built at Camulodunum within the old Catuvellaunian defensive dykes, but its harbour was several miles away at Fingringhoe on the estuary of the River Colne. Similarly Exeter, where a military fort is known, was provided with harbour installations on the Exe, three miles down-stream near the deeper water.

The presence of military remains at Fishbourne and Chichester dating to the time of the invasion, raises a number of interesting strategic and political questions. While it could be argued that a small peace-keeping force would have been advantageous to Cogidubnus at the beginning of the occupation, the excavated remains suggest something far more substantial. But as we have argued above, it is highly unlikely that a major landing would have been made so far west as part of the original invasion

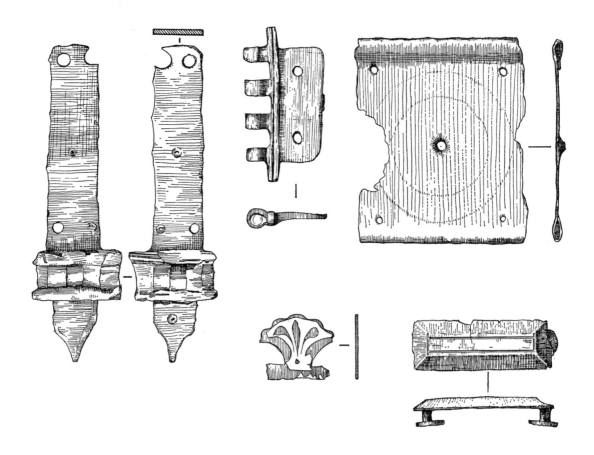

plan. A far more likely context for the military structures is offered by
the second stage of the invasion, the conquest of the hostile south-west
by the second legion led by Vespasian, an event which must have followed hard upon the initial thrust to Camulodunum.

The historian Suetonius provides a brief account of these events. [15]
Vespasian and his legion, we are told, took the Isle of Wight, overcame
two powerful tribes and destroyed more than twenty fortified native
capitals. At what stage this happened is not exactly clear, but Vespasian
was present at the battle of the Medway, from which the native leader
Caratacus fled to stir up trouble in the west. It could well have been at
this stage that the *legio II augusta* was detached to prevent any serious up-
rising on the flank at such a vital moment in the advance. Alternatively,
if the flight of Caratacus was not viewed as a serious threat, Vespasian's
departure might have been delayed until after the capitulation of Camulodunum. At any event, within a few weeks of the landing Vespasian was
tackling the tribes of the south-west. For this the friendly enclave of
Cogidubnus' kingdom would have been of enormous value, the more

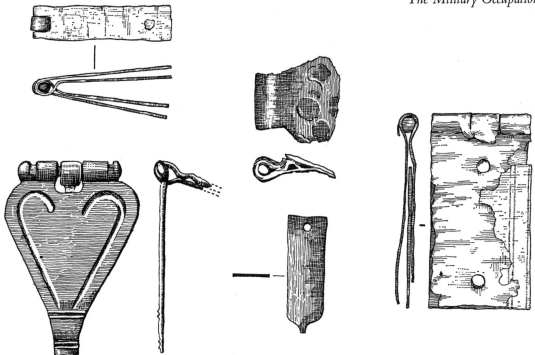

6   *Bronze fittings from military equipment*

so because of its excellent harbours protected from the winds and storms
coming from the south by the land-mass of the Isle of Wight. Good harbours would have been essential because any conquest of south-western
Britain would have entailed the use of extensive naval support to bring
up troops and supplies to the line of battle. The advance would have been
something like a complex pincer movement. Exactly the same tactics
were used by the commander Agricola 35 years later in his conquest of
eastern Scotland, where Tacitus tells us the enemy were thrown into confusion by being caught between the army on one side and the navy on
the other. Sometimes, he says, the mariners and soldiers would meet in
the same camps at night and exchange stories.[16] We must not, however,
over-emphasise the fighting significance of the navy in Vespasian's campaign; it was essentially a means of rapidly transporting reinforcements
to where they were most needed.

One possible explanation for the Fishbourne and Chichester remains lies,
therefore, in their construction and use by Vespasian as his principal supply base from which those further west could be served, bases such as those

known to be at Hamworthy in Poole harbour, at Topsham near Exeter, and the suspected bases near Weymouth and at Bitterne. The Fishbourne store buildings close to the harbour would have been suitable for the protection of corn and other commodities in transit, whilst the remains beneath Chichester might have belonged to a camp for reserve troops or even the winter quarters to which the field army could withdraw at the end of the first season's campaign. This, of course, is speculative but it has the advantage of explaining the observed facts in terms of their broader significance. Little advance can be made, however, until the work at Fishbourne is extended and more facts are available from Chichester.

Vespasian's campaign against the Durotriges and probably the Dumnonii, the tribes occupying west Hampshire, Dorset, south Somerset and Devon, and the destruction of their principal fortified settlements was probably rapid and may well have been accomplished within the first two campaigning seasons, but the situation was an uneasy one and forts such as those at Hod Hill, Waddon Hill and elsewhere had to be built for the permanent garrisons left to keep an eye on the native tribesmen.

By 47, south-east Britain was regarded as conquered and a densely fortified frontier zone had been constructed on either side of the Fosseway – a military communication road running from Lincoln to the Devon coast east of Exeter. Even though the forts remained in Durotrigian territory, it is most unlikely that the installations of Fishbourne and Chichester were required any longer – the new network of inland communications would have rendered them obsolete and the land they occupied could have been returned to its original owners.

IV

Civil Development: Claudius to Nero

When the army finally moved away from the area, they left behind them a well fitted harbour at Fishbourne and an excellent system of roads converging on Chichester, for it is probable that Stane Street, the road linking Chichester to London, and the coast road west from Chichester were laid out initially by the military authorities. The presence of the army would also have encouraged camp followers to set up their stalls nearby, providing for the needs of the soldiers, at a price. The military presence, then, created a situation favourable to urban growth and as soon as the soldiers moved off civilian development began to flourish. Similar processes lay behind the growth of many of the Roman towns in England and on the Continent.

How long it took the new developments at Chichester to usurp the position of the old market at Selsey it is difficult yet to say, but we must imagine a steady drift towards the new centre. Archaeology has little yet to show of the early stages in the growth of the town, but some of the streets would have been laid out, flanked by timber buildings, traces of which have turned up on the east side of North Street. A substantial masonry building found in 1740 at the corner of St Martins Lane and East Street may also be of this early date, for lying in the rubble was found an inscription of well cut letters carved on a slab of Purbeck marble 3 ft by $2^1/_2$ ft.[17] Although it has since been lost, the lettering is recorded to have read 'For Nero Claudius Caesar Augustus, son of the deified Claudius, grandson of Germanicus Caesar, great grandson of Tiberius Caesar Augustus, great great grandson of the deified Augustus, in his fourth year of Tribunician power, four times acclaimed Imperator, consul for the fourth time by decree of the Senate, the vow was deservedly fulfilled.' The stone, a dedicatory inscription, is an impressive tribute by the young town to the emperor Nero. It may well be a result of Cogidubnus' go-ahead policy of forcing Romanization on his people. The inscription alone shows that by the year 58 the community was fast developing a decidedly Roman aspect.

At Fishbourne the changes can be more closely followed. One of the first alterations to be made to the military layout was to the road system. The southern road was abandoned and the ford by which it crossed the stream was dug away to allow the stream to flow faster in order to improve the drainage of the valley above. The northern road, however, was retained but because of the dampness of the land hereabouts side ditches were dug along part of its length to remove surface water and drain it into the stream. At the stream-crossing a timber bridge was provided. It

Plate 8

was a simple affair based on two flanking rows of oak piles, 9 ins in diameter, rammed into the ground on either side of the main stream channel to serve as revetments, behind which the rubble and gravel of the causeways was piled. On top of each row of timbers a single horizontal beam would have been placed to serve as the base for the thick planks which would have spanned the eleven-foot gap between the rows. The bridge itself was quite narrow, barely 10 ft wide, but a ford was provided by the side of it, perhaps to allow livestock and wheeled traffic to pass while pedestrians could walk more comfortably across the bridge.

Fig. 7

The principal building activity was concentrated in the area east of the stream, partly over the site of one of the old military store buildings. Here two completely new timber buildings were erected, both built on a framework of sill beams about a foot square, placed on the ground surface. Into these would have been slotted the vertical timbers which made up the framework of the superstructure and between them walls of

Fig. 8

wattle and daub would have been inserted. Of the two buildings which have been almost totally excavated, the southern (building 4) was by far the more impressive with its seven rooms laid out in a single block 18 ft wide by more than 60 ft long and flanked along part of the east side by a veranda. Each room had been carefully floored with mortar or clay and some, at least, of the walls had been thinly plastered and painted red and white.

The building which lay to the north was different both in style and function. It was composed simply of a range of five rooms constructed end on in a strip 10 ft wide with two much larger rooms built across the north end to give a T-shaped ground plan. East of the range was a large working area which ran the length of the building and was probably roofed in one with it. The entrance to the working area lay towards its centre where stones and tiles were thrown down to prevent the constant tread of feet wearing the soil into hollows, which would soon have become puddles in wet weather. There is some evidence to suggest that a

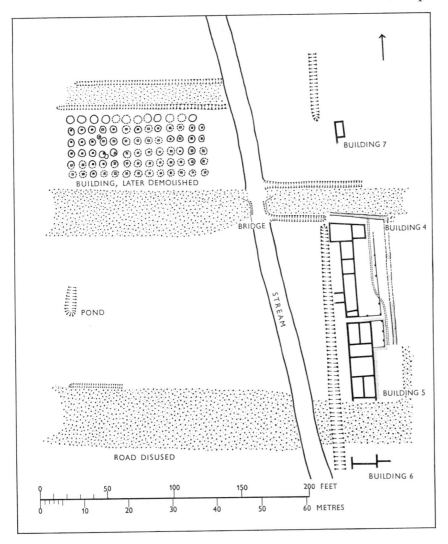

7   *The arrangement of the Neronian civil buildings*

passage-way led through the building opposite the entrance and gave
access to what appears to be a bridge, constructed of massive horizontal
timbers, over a wide drainage gully which ran the length of the building.

The rooms of the main range were floored with mortar and clay, but
there was no trace of wall painting. The working area in front was un-
floored except for the rubble spread, but within the enclosure was a small
oven with a fuel pit close by and near the oven was found a large lump
of crude bronze, hinting at the possibility of bronze-working.

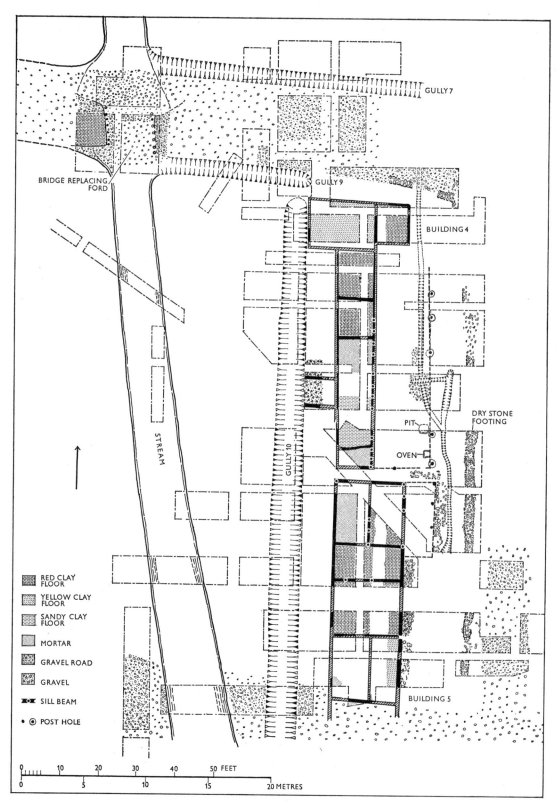

GULLY 7

BRIDGE REPLACING
FORD

GULLY 9

BUILDING 4

STREAM

GULLY 10

PIT

OVEN

DRY STONE
FOOTING

RED CLAY
FLOOR

YELLOW CLAY
FLOOR

SANDY CLAY
FLOOR

MORTAR

GRAVEL ROAD

GRAVEL

SILL BEAM

POST HOLE

BUILDING 5

0	10	20	30	40	50 FEET
0	5		10	15	20 METRES

8   Timber buildings 4 and 5 – the first timber house

Although the two buildings were separated from each other by a narrow passageway, they are clearly part of a unified plan, for both were fronted by a drystone footing more than 3 ft wide, outside of which lay a north-south street. Exactly how the footing functioned it is difficult to say, but it may well have supported a continuous colonnade of timber or brick serving to unify the two structures. Similar colonnades, common to several buildings, are a well known feature of Roman street architecture in this country. A close parallel is provided by a row of early timber shops in the Roman town of Verulamium:[18] their frontage onto Watling Street was lined by a spacious veranda which allowed pedestrians to walk for some distance under cover. A second unifying feature at Fishbourne was a wide drainage gully which ran the full length of the two buildings and must eventually have emptied into the stream.

The two buildings, then, are part of the same overall plan but are evidently of different functions. The southern building with its spacious rooms, painted walls and veranda would have been eminently suitable as a high class dwelling, while the northern building was some kind of work-shop with attached living quarters. It is tempting to see them as the main house and servants' range belonging to a single establishment of some status. By later standards the accommodation was somewhat meagre, but compared with contemporary Romano-British buildings the Fishbourne complex was positively luxurious. The problems of ownership are perhaps better left for a later chapter (pp. 165–9).

Fig. 9

In addition to the two buildings just described, part of another of some size was found to the south of the road (unless, of course, it is part of building 4). Clearly Fishbourne in the 50's and early 60's was fairly densely built-up.

On the north side of the northern road stood the military store building, which by this time was no longer of much use. The main problem was that timber imbedded in the ground tended to rot through just above ground-level, where the dampness and the supply of air were optimum for the activities of the bacteria which destroy wood cells. An excellent example of just this process was provided by the barn in the farmyard at the south edge of the site, built in 1918–19. Within about 20 years some of its foot-thick uprights had been so eaten through by bacteria that supporting slabs of concrete had to be cast around them to keep the building up. This is precisely the type of problem that would have presented itself in the 50's and 60's of the first century. Some of the uprights had completely rotted through and were removed, leaving stumps in position.

Others, however, were still sufficiently sound to warrant digging out. In the case of the first it is possible to recognize the earth-filled void created by the stump rotting, while digging out is represented by a large demolition pit dug through the original construction pit. Both states can be simply traced by excavation. Sometime, then, probably late in the 50's, the store building was demolished and its site and that of the road to the north became blanketed with a thick layer of occupation refuse thrown out from the buildings to the south and east.

Immediately to the east of the old store house was a low-lying area alongside the stream. Several attempts were made to consolidate it with tips of stone and gravel but it remained open, perhaps as a yard. Further to the east, on drier land, a small timber building or shed was built, attached to a boundary fence, neither of which have been fully traced.

The area further to the north along the valley was evidently occupied by timber buildings, but excavations here have been confined to very limited trial trenching. How extensively this area was built up remains to be demonstrated, but at one point a timber-lined well was discovered. The mere existence of such a feature implies nearby habitation, but details must await large-scale excavation.

One final feature requires comment. In the north-west corner of the site a substantial ditch was found, measuring some 12 ft wide and up to 6 ft deep. It turned a right-angle beneath what was later to become the west end of the North Wing of the palace. Why so large a ditch was dug is not clear, nor can its extent be traced any further. At first a military origin seemed possible, but the pottery found in the primary silt of the ditch showed that it was open in the Neronian period, by which time the military occupation of the site had ceased. It may, perhaps, have served as a property boundary or for drainage, or a combination of the two.

The harbour to the south still played an important part in the life of the site. At this stage ships were coming in and jettisoning their ballast of stone boulders before taking on heavy cargoes. These boulders have been found in some numbers in the early levels and when identified they prove to derive mainly from the western seaways, coming from Cornwall, the Channel Islands and probably the Armorican peninsula, showing that much of Fishbourne's overseas trade lay with these western areas, an idea which gains some support from a study of the imported pottery.

It can be said, therefore, that in the decade or two following the invasion, Fishbourne and Chichester developed rapidly from their early military beginnings, Chichester taking on the form of a small urban centre, while Fishbourne continued to serve as its port. At Fishbourne, however, there developed a large private house which by the local standards of the time must have belonged to a person of some wealth. Whether it stood alone amid the harbour installations or is one of a group of private dwellings is a question which can only be answered by further extensive excavations.

V

The Proto-palace

Early in the 60's, during the reign of Nero, a significant change took place at Fishbourne: the timber house and its outbuildings were pulled down and replaced by a substantial masonry building planned in Roman style – called here the proto-palace for reasons which will later become evident. Fortunately, it is possible to trace in some detail how the preparations were made for the building and how gradually it took shape.

At an early stage, but possibly not right at the beginning, the timber buildings were demolished, any useful materials such as roof-tiles or timbers being stockpiled for later use. The ground sills upon which the old structure was based were apparently too rotten to warrant removal: one of them could still be traced in position, surviving now as a streak of brown spongy soil. The clay daub from the walls was generally spread about to level up the old site. It was at this stage that the stream was diverted into a new channel dug along the eastern limit of the building site, along the line now followed by the present-day stream. Its original bed was completely filled with clay and rubble derived from the building works. The next stage was the reconstruction of the southern road by remetalling the part passing across the gully and stream, and considerably widening it west of the stream. This road and the north-south road, which was also partly remetalled at this time, were used as the main service roads connected with the building work. Along them the building materials would have been brought in and, judging by the thickness of greensand chippings lying above the metalling, the ashlar blocks were probably tooled here and piled up for when the builders needed them.

The area of the old timber buildings and the expanse of open land to the west was now enclosed by a fence constructed of large vertical timbers placed in individual post-pits. One row, running north–south, has been traced close to the eastern limit of the site. The second row, which joined it at approximately right-angles, ran along the southern side of the northern road, actually impinging upon the metalling. That the fence belongs to this period can be shown by the way in which its post-holes are cut through the destroyed walls and sill beams of the old building, while the posts were packed in position with large fresh blocks of stone of the type brought in to provide the decorative finishes to the new masonry proto-palace. Within this fenced enclosure a shallow scoop-like excavation had been made down to below the water-table, to provide what appears to be a pond. It is tempting therefore to suggest that one function of the enclosure was to retain livestock, and since the stream was now filled-in a pond had to be dug to provide water for the animals.

It was within the eastern part of the enclosure that much of the preparation work for the new building was carried out. The masons responsible for creating the decorative stone inlay used the area as their working yard, leaving behind them a thick litter of stone chippings, sand and partly finished objects, which provide a unique insight into the processes used by the stone workers. Several types of stone were brought in as crude blocks, the commonest being a blue-grey Purbeck marble from Dorset, a hard white chalk which probably also came from the Purbeck hills in Dorset, a grey silt-stone probably from the Weald and a red silt-stone which has been identified as coming from somewhere around the Mediterranean. This particular stone is a laminated sedimentary rock, streaks of which are sometimes yellow or purple, colours which also proved to be attractive to the stone workers. Granular white Carrara marble from Italy was also imported at this time though in much smaller quantities, largely because of the expense, but a brown speckled marble from the Côte d'Or in eastern France occurred in relatively large amounts.

First of all the crude blocks of stone were tooled into regular shapes using a hammer to begin with and later various grades of chisels, ending up with an all-over pecking with a fine chisel point. Then followed the sawing of the blocks into sheets of various thicknesses ranging between an eighth of an inch to three-quarters of an inch. Pliny describes how this was carried out with a large multiple-bladed saw which cut a single block into a number of sheets in one operation. The iron saw blades were not generally toothed, a toothed blade would wear out too quickly. Instead strips of iron were used with a fine sand as an abrasive and water to lubricate the process. The sand grains rubbed backwards and forwards by the blades would soon cut deeply into the stone. Pliny also mentions how some dishonest masons used a coarse sand to make wider cuts and thus used up the client's marble more quickly. That these processes were employed at Fishbourne is shown by the thick layers of fine white sand found all over the floor of the working area and by several broken blocks of stone which show the marks of the multiple-bladed saw.

Fig. 10

Plate 12

61

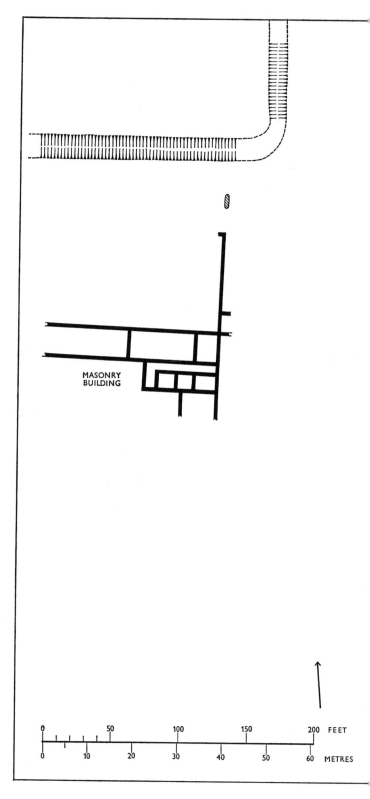

10 The arrangement of the buildings c. AD 70

MASONRY
BUILDING

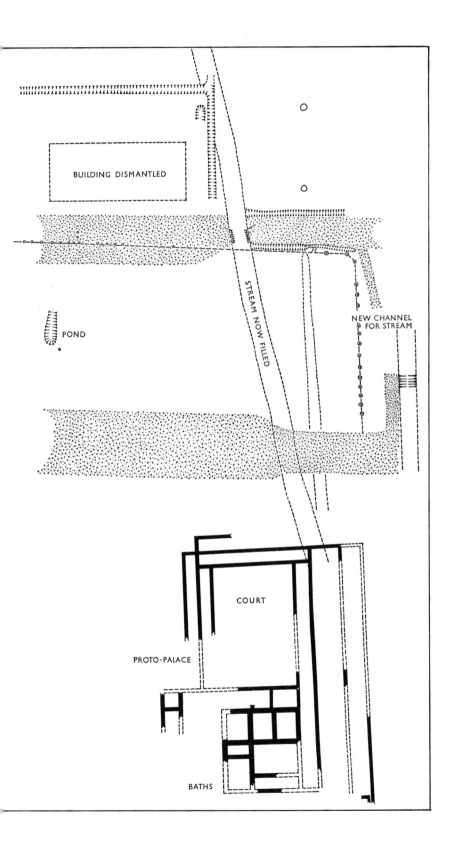

BUILDING DISMANTLED

POND

STREAM NOW FILLED

NEW CHANNEL
FOR STREAM

COURT

PROTO-PALACE

BATHS

After the sheet of stone had been produced, its upper surface was carefully smoothed, using rubbers of a hard iron-stone, several of which still survive. Then the sheet was marked out with a scriber into the required shape. If, as was often the case with the Purbeck marble, the sheet was to be cut into strips or squares, the scribed line was usually pecked with a chisel to form a keying for the saw, a single-bladed saw this time, which was used to cut along the line. Usually the saw was kept horizontal to the surface of the stone to give a much straighter line. When it was nearly through, a quick hammer blow would detach the strip, leaving a burr along one edge (rather like breaking a bar of chocolate), which could easily be trimmed off with a hammer.

The general process, most commonly employed, has been outlined but it must be remembered that a wide variety of products were turned out by the yard. In addition to strips and geometric shapes of stone for floor inlay, marble mouldings were carved from Purbeck and Carrara marble for use in framing windows and doors. One area of the yard seems to have specialized in cutting small intricate shapes for a very fine inlay, probably for furniture, while in another area Purbeck marble mortars and pestles were being produced for use in the kitchen. In fact the masons were making the entire range of stone fittings for the new house, which was by this stage taking shape close by.

It is most likely that the yard was used by other craftsmen as well, such as the carpenters, whose contribution to the new building would have been no less than that of the masons. Little trace of their activities could, however, be expected to survive. In one area close to the masons, large lumps of iron slag suggest the proximity of iron smiths making the nails and other fittings which would have been necessary, particularly for the complicated roof structure. Other products, like roof-tiles and bricks, would have been made in clamps close to the clay pits, such as those at Dell Quay, just south of Fishbourne, and would have been brought up to the building site as finished products.

While all these preparations were going on, the house itself was gradually rising, built in a fine ashlar masonry of greensand blocks set in hard cream-coloured mortar on footings of coursed stone blocks placed dry in wide foundation trenches.

The building now lies partly beneath the modern main road (the A 27) and partly beneath houses and farm buildings on either side, but gradually, by means of trial trenches dug in the gardens during the winter months when the flowers had died off and by rather more extensive excavation in the old farmyard, it has been possible to piece together the main outlines of the building. Originally it covered an area of 190 ft by more than 150 ft and was composed of four main elements: a large colonnaded garden, a bath suite, a range of living rooms and a block of servants' quarters and work-rooms.

The garden, which lay on the north side, was enclosed on at least three sides, and possibly on the fourth, by a veranda which on the west and north was double. Although only the footings survive, it is probable that it was provided with a colonnade on the garden side based on a ground-level stylobate (a foundation of large stone blocks). A number of fragments of column drums made from greensand have been found belonging to this early period. Several of them have a roughened surface which might imply that they were originally furnished with a surfacing of stucco, indeed this is likely because the greensand, if exposed to weathering, would have flaked very badly. Other columns seem to have been built up in a normal Roman fashion with quadrant or semicircular tiles and segments of stone which would have been mortared together and coated with stucco. Although none occurred in position, the individual elements were found lying about in building and rubble layers in some quantity.

When the garden of the main Flavian palace was being excavated, a large number of pieces of carved stone were found, used as packing for posts set up in the garden. These fragments clearly belonged to an earlier structure, but it was not for some time after jigsaw-puzzling them together that we realized that they were the excrescences knocked off very ornate Corinthian capitals. These Corinthian capitals were very probably derived from the proto-palace and may well have been used somewhere in the garden, if not on the actual garden colonnades. The carving of the capitals is very lively and quite accomplished with elaborate ram's horn volutes projecting from each corner, faces wreathed in oak leaves between them and luxurious foliage below. It is surprising to find so much variety and assurance in carving at such an early date in the provinces, but parallels to most of the elements can be found in first-century work in Italy. Their very existence at Fishbourne must imply the presence of continental craftsmen.

Plates 13, 14

The living rooms were laid out in a single range of nearly 200 ft along the veranda flanking the east side of the garden. Although the main walls have been defined, excavation has been so limited that practically nothing of the interiors or even the sizes of the individual rooms is known, but

Fig. 11

originally they must have been very elaborately decorated. Some evidence for this comes from the layers of rubble derived from the superstructure of the building when, a few years later, it was drastically modified and new floors inserted at a much higher level. The rubble consists of the remains of destroyed walls of wattle and daub which had been thickly plastered and painted. They were probably the partition walls of the rooms dismantled during the alterations. The painted plaster, though now broken into fragments, gives a very clear idea of the high standard of interior decoration. Basically the walls were divided into three zones, a lower dado about 3 ft high, then the main wall panels, topped by a painted cornice, and finally a plain white frieze. The dado was painted with a dark blue-black background over which leaves and flowers were painted with bold brush strokes of green, yellow and white. Above the dado the wall was divided into rectangular panels painted red, yellow and deep blue, enclosed in a plain white frame line and enlivened with another, coloured, frame line, usually about 2 ins in from the edge, yellow on the deep blue, white on the red and brown on the yellow. These panels were painted on a bright blue-green background which was allowed to appear in wide strips around them, over-painted with elegant stylized floral designs in white with the occasional use of red and yellow. The cornice, which capped the panels, was an accomplished piece of perspective painting, giving the impression of a delicate moulding seen in the warm light of evening. While most of the painted fragments fall within this general range, other pieces in purples and ochres are known.

Some of the walls were visually divided by fluted pilasters made from stucco, an arrangement popular in Italy in the first century but so far unknown in Britain. The painting as well as the stucco work is of an extremely high standard, it is most unlikely that any native in Britain was skilled in these arts at such an early date. Again, therefore, it is necessary to suppose that foreign craftsmen were brought in.

No primary floors have been found in position in this part of the proto-palace, but the activity of the masons and their waste material mentioned above gives a good idea of what the floors were originally like. Apart from plain mortar, two finishes were in use: normal mosaic work using black and white tesserae and *opus sectile*. This entailed the construction of elaborate patterns from geometric shapes of coloured stone, here mainly red, blue and white with some grey and yellow. *Opus sectile* floors were widespread in Italy and southern Gaul, but as a decorative technique it

Plate 11

66

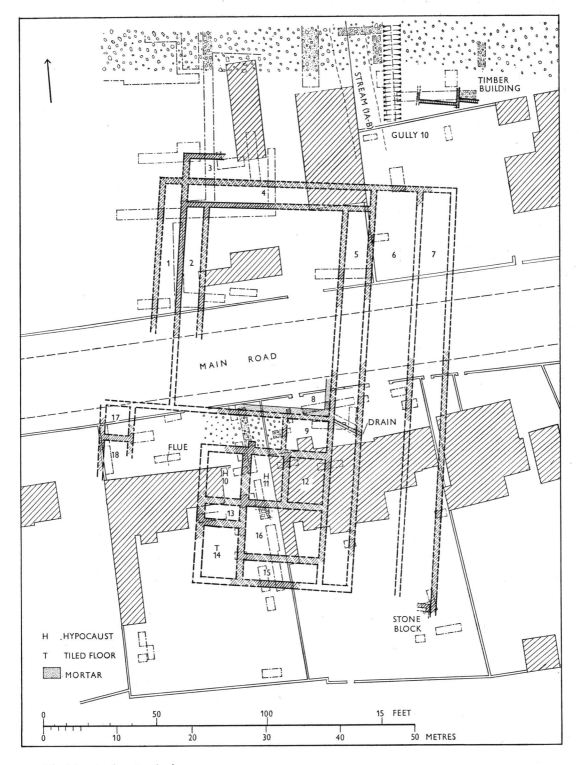

Labels within the figure:

TIMBER BUILDING

STREAM (1A-B)

GULLY 10

3

4

1 2

5 6 7

8

17

18

FLUE

9

H 10

H 11

12

13

T 14

16

15

MAIN ROAD

DRAIN

STONE BLOCK

H   HYPOCAUST
T   TILED FLOOR
     MORTAR

0   50   100   15 FEET

0   10   20   30   40   50 METRES

11   *The Neronian 'proto-palace'*

does not seem to have appealed to the Romano-Britons since very few examples are known in this country.

The third structural element of the proto-palace was the bath block which lay to the south of the courtyard. It was simple but effective, consisting of two separate parts: a cold swimming bath and a suite of heated rooms, joined only by a heated ante-room (no. 9), which probably served as an entrance chamber as well. The swimming bath only just projects into the area available for excavation; the rest of it now lies beneath the main road. All that survives is the corner, showing a bench of masonry, rendered with pink mortar, built around the wall of the room; the floor, which was probably of pink mortar as well, has been destroyed, but the outfall drain which led the waste water away shows that the bath must have been at least 3 ft deep.

The heated suite is more complex, consisting of at least seven rooms, of which four (nos 10–12, 16) were heated by means of hypocausts from stoking chambers on the north or west side of the block. The three rooms closest to the heat source (nos 10–12) were probably *caldaria*, rooms of intense heat where the occupant would have sweated profusely in the steamy atmosphere, scraping his skin clean with a strigil. It is difficult to be sure, but in all probability the rooms were heated to different temperatures and at least one of them may originally have been fitted with a hot bath provided with scalding water from a boiler built over one of the stokeries. None of these details, however, survive. Attached to the centre *caldarium* was a large square room (no. 16) of somewhat gentler heat (the *tepidarium*). Part of its sub-floor structure survives, showing the emplacement of a semicircular plunge bath built against its north wall. The bathers could either rest in the warm atmosphere of the room or dip into the tepid water of the bath.

The room which opened out at the south-west corner of the *tepidarium* (no. 14) was floored with tiles and there is some evidence to suggest that a tiled bench had been built against the north wall, unfortunately further excavation was not possible here, but it may well have been the cold room (*frigidarium*). Of the other two rooms defined by the excavation, there is little to be said except that they probably served as corridors, but how the suite linked onto the main range cannot now be defined.

Although the excavation was necessarily limited to a few small trial trenches dug in the flower beds of attractively laid-out gardens, a great deal of the Roman ground plan has been recovered. The rooms, however, had all been extensively robbed of their building materials late in the Roman period and practically nothing of the superstructure survives. How the walls were jacketed with box tiles to lead the hot air through, and how the rooms were roofed are problems to which no firm answers can ever be given. Nevertheless the footings of the heated part of the bath suite were far more substantial than those in other parts of the proto-palace, a fact which implies that they were capable of supporting a much greater weight, presumably that of the masonry vaults with which the baths were probably roofed. Masonry vaulting had several advantages over timber in these contexts: it would not warp in the steamy atmosphere, it retained the heat more efficiently and it considerably reduced the risk of fire. We may tentatively assume, therefore, that the baths were vaulted, perhaps with two parallel east-west tunnels built of hollow box-tiles and concrete. A few fragments of voussoir-shaped box-tiles found in the destruction rubble add support to the view. It is difficult to know how the baths would have looked from the outside. If the well preserved Hunting Baths at Lepcis Magna[19] offer a guide, we must suppose that the vaults were left uncovered as bare concrete, but in a British climate it may have been necessary to clothe the masonry beneath a protective pitched roof of tiles.

The fourth part of the proto-palace is a group of rooms, of which only two are known, lying to the west of the baths and extending into an unexcavated area. Positive identification is impossible, but they may well have formed part of the servants' quarters, tucked out of sight but conveniently linked by passageways to the main building and close to the stoking chambers of the baths.

In the context of what had gone before at Fishbourne, the proto-palace was architecturally a great advance, its very structure implies the attentions of a large number of foreign specialists well versed in constructional and decorative arts. When functions and residential space are considered, however, it is not so dissimilar to the earlier timber house. The main range of rooms with its fronting veranda is repeated in both, and both have ample room for servants. The difference lies in the addition of luxuries such as the colonnaded courtyard and the baths. It is the very existence of these purely Roman luxuries, together with the quality of the internal decoration, which underlines the change in status between the two buildings. It is probably correct to consider them together because the proto-palace does seem to replace the timber house in so far as the timber buildings were still standing while the shell of the proto-palace was being erected, and were not demolished until the time had come for the final decorative touches to be added. In all probability the change marks a major advance in the wealth of status of the owning family, but these points must be reserved for later discussion.

The proto-palace is not unique even in Sussex, for only 16 miles to the east, at Angmering, part of a closely similar building has been excavated,[20] incorporating many of the same architectural skills and evidently drawing on the same sources of supply for the raw materials. The tiles used in the two buildings are identical and Angmering has produced a number of *opus sectile* elements similar in material and shape to those from Fishbourne. The parallels between the two are so close that they must have been constructed largely by the same labour force. Indeed, it may well have been profitable for a team of continental designers and builders to seek their fortunes in the prosperous pro-Roman territory of Cogidubnus. There must have been many aristocrats in the area only too ready to sink some capital in these expensive Roman luxuries, now that Roman government was here to stay. The Roman villas at Southwick, Wiggonholt and Pulborough all have interesting preculiarities in their designs which set them apart from the normal Romano-British villa development.[21] Perhaps they, too, began in this early period.

While the proto-palace was in use, new developments were underway on the high ground to the west. After a shallow ditch which ran across the site had been filled in, work began on the construction of a very substantial masonry building. Unfortunately, only the corner of it projects into the land available for excavation, but enough to show that it consisted of two ranges of rooms joining at right-angles with another group of three rooms, linked by an L-shaped corridor, at the junction of the ranges. From the plan alone, the building must have been intended to be one of some importance, but it was never completed above foundation level. Instead, a stone-built culvert was cut raggedly through two of the footings and the site left open. Possibly we are looking here at the results of a change in building plans: it may be that the whole project was abandoned or that part of the building only was erected, the culvert belonging to it. The problem cannot be resolved without further excavation beneath the modern houses and gardens which now cover the crucial area, but one thing is certain – within a very short time this site was to be used for the West Wing of the great Flavian palace, while the proto-palace 300 ft away was to be incorporated in the East Wing of the same concept. Changes were in the air and new schemes of staggering size were being prepared.

Plate 10

VI

The Buildings of the Flavian Palace

It was sometime between AD 75 and 80 that the construction of the great Palace began, a few years after Vespasian became Emperor in 69, founding what is known as the Flavian dynasty. The dating of the initial stages of the building depends upon the pottery and coins found sealed in and beneath its floor levels. A relatively large collection of coins, including a number issued during the early part of Vespasian's reign, and none dating after the year 73, were found below the floors. Clearly, then, building cannot have begun before 73 and, judging by the relatively unworn state of the latest issues, it must have started soon after, before the coins had been long in circulation. The imported samian pottery from beneath the floor levels is similarly helpful: the latest vessels, large, highly decorated bowls, were made in the same Gaulish factories as an important group found in one of the shops in Pompeii buried by the eruption of Vesuvius in AD 79. These vessels, commonly in use throughout the Roman world, therefore support the dating of the coins and indicate that the main building activity at Fishbourne took place in the second half of the 70's. The very latest of the construction levels of the Palace, the garden surfaces and the upper metalling of the service road, produced two coins of Vespasian's successor, Domitian, which show that the finishing touches were being made to the Palace in the 80's. The whole project, then, must have taken at least five years to complete, which is hardly surprising considering its enormous size.

The architects, who first surveyed the site, were faced with a problem: the land sloped down to the old filled-in stream bed, from about 26 ft Ordnance Datum at the west to 15 OD at the lowest point. It also sloped to the south towards the harbour. In spite of the digging of a number of drainage gullies in the preceding period and the re-routing of the stream, the lowlying areas were still damp and ill-drained. The solution was simple – a complete levelling of the entire site. In practice this meant that the western part of the site was left at its original level of 25 ft OD, and a vast artificial terrace was created to the east at a height of about 20 ft OD, covering an area of 400 ft by 900 ft. This involved altogether the removal

Fig. 12

of more than 36,000 cubic yards of clay and gravel from the west part of the area and its dumping over the eastern part.

The actual progress of the work was of course more complicated. For example, to cover the eastern part of the site with 5 ft of clay and gravel and then to attempt to put up a building on it would have been nonsense.

12   *The present village of New Fishbourne, with the area of the Roman Palace stippled. The main road is the A 27*

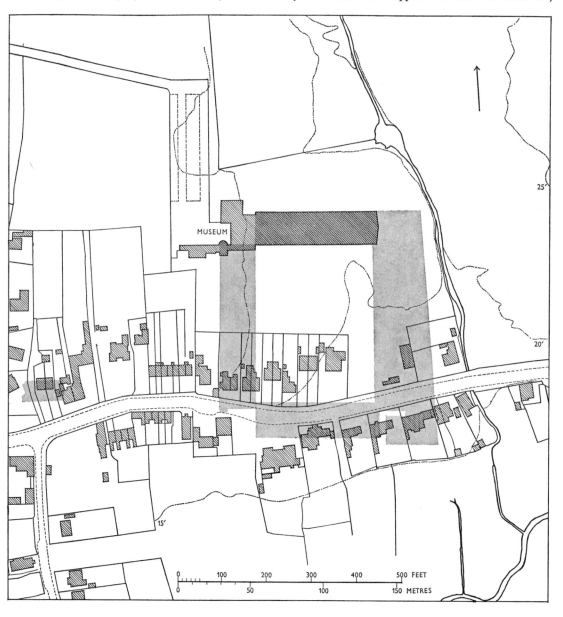

What in practice the Roman builders did was to dig the foundation trenches first, throwing the spoil out into the areas between the walls, and then to lay their concrete footings. When these had set they began to build the freestanding part of the ashlar superstructure, allowing splashes of mortar and chippings from the tooling of the blocks to accumulate in heaps within the rooms. Only after this stage had been completed was the clay and rubble brought in from outside and spread around, up to the required level. The saving in time and labour allowed by this simple piece of forward planning was enormous. Problems arose with the existing proto-palace because its floor levels related to the original ground surface and not the newly created one, but these were simply overcome by disregarding all earlier floors and raising the entire level of the old building, using the remains of its demolished wattle and daub walls in the levelling process.

The acquisition of the building materials needed for the entire complex implies a minor masterpiece of organization. To give some idea of what was involved, we must consider a single stretch of wall. First of all a foundation trench was dug into the solid clay, some $2^1/_2$ ft wide and of about the same depth. Into the bottom of this pairs of oak piles, 3 ft long and about 6 ins in diameter, were rammed every foot, so that the walls of a single average-sized room would have needed between 150 and 200 piles. The foundation trenches were then filled with flints set in concrete and above this the superstructure, consisting of walls $1^1/_2$–2 ft thick built of squared green-sand blocks, was erected to the full height of the single-storied building. In all some two miles of walling were built.

Two types of basic building stone were used, greensand and Mixon limestone. The greensand, geologically Upper Greensand from below the chalk, probably came from the Weald near Pulborough, conveniently close for Stane Street to provide easy road transport. This type of stone was used for all but the West Wing of the Palace which was built of blocks of a coarse limestone, from the Mixon reef off Selsey Bill, many of them water eroded slabs collected from near the tide level. All the gardens of the Palace were surrounded by colonnades based on a foundation of large stone blocks, called a stylobate, and fronted by a continuous ground level stone gutter. The structural and visual implications of these colonnades will be considered later – here we are concerned with the stone. The gutter blocks, each about 3 ft wide, 4 ft long and 2 ft thick, were of two different stones: a greenish sandstone of a type found in a reef off Bracklesham, a few miles south of Chichester, and a fossiliferous limestone found outcropping on the cliffs at Bembridge in the Isle of Wight. The stylobate blocks were all of Bembridge limestone. It is interesting that both outcrops should be close to the sea: sea transport was easy and cheap and Fishbourne with its harbour was ideally suited to be supplied by boat.

The columns, of which there were more than 160, were made from various limestones including an oolitic stone from Gloucestershire and Caen stone from Northern France. Such wide-flung connections show that the masons were in a position to choose carefully the stone most suited to the job.

The roofing of the building would have required colossal quantities of timber, presumably cut in the nearby oak forests of the coastal plain, as well as many tons of iron nails. The roof covering was of the standard *imbrex* and *tegulae* tiles, probably made at Dell Quay, two miles to the south on the edge of the Fishbourne inlet, where extensive remains of Roman tile production have come to light. Finally, many hundreds of tons of lime-mortar were used, made by burning chalk from the nearby Downs and mixing the lime thus formed with a pebbly flint aggregate derived from the gravel deposits east of Chichester.

For the basic structure alone the problem of shipping correct quantities of materials at the right stage of the building programme must have been enormous, not least because many of the sources were being exploited for the first time, presumably by native labour quite unused to building in masonry. The logistics of man management alone would have been enough to frighten many a modern clerk of works into a nervous decline.

Governing all these issues of the supply of materials and of labour was the basic plan to which the architects were working. The Palace was to consist of four residential ranges arranged around a large central garden 250 ft by 320 ft, while to the south was to be a second garden of comparable size leading down to the sea. Everything faced east towards Chichester, to which the site was already linked by the existing southern road, belonging initially to the military period. To the west, behind the main Palace, were to be the servants' quarters and other domestic installations. Everything was well thought out and planned in advance. While different phases in the building programme can be distinguished, the entire concept is evidently of one period, excepting of course the earlier proto-palace which was incorporated into the south-east corner.

The basic principles behind the design were simple. A central east-west axis was created projecting the line of the road, and astride this, in the

Fig. 13

East Wing, the entrance hall was built. The axis was continued across the garden as a hedge-lined path and ended up in front of the audience chamber built in the centre of the West Wing. About this axis the building was arranged as symmetrically as possible. The entrance hall, garden and West Wing functioned as a single unit, all three elements being in

13   Plan of the Flavian Palace and its formal garden

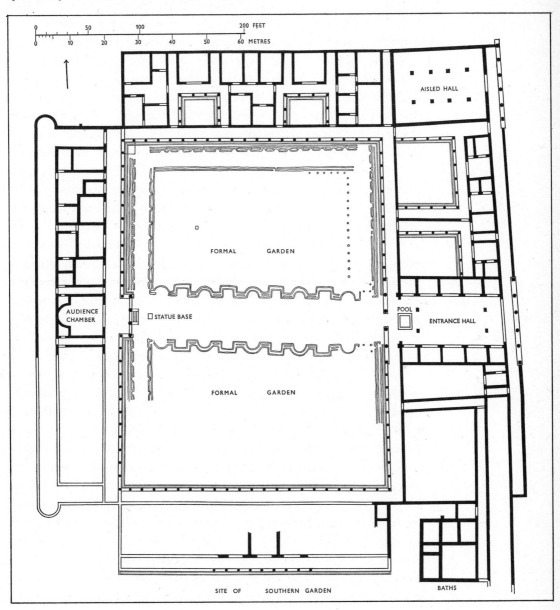

easy visual and physical communication and linked to the outside world, whilst the North and South Wings and the remaining parts of the East Wing were essentially private environments in-turned upon themselves.

The West Wing

Fig. 14

The West Wing was the visual and functional centrepiece of the design. It was the first part of the building to be seen in its entirety by a visitor, and it was here that the principal administrative rooms lay. The wing was given an added grandeur by being built on the upper (25 ft OD) terrace while the ground level of the garden and the rest of the Palace in front of it was at least 5 ft lower. The change in level was revetted by a masonry wall, the top of which, on a level with the West Wing floors, served as a stylobate for the fronting colonnade. Behind this colonnade, more than 330 ft long, lay the range of rooms, of which more than half now lie within the area available for excavation. If the arrangement was symmetrical about the centre line, there would originally have been about 27 rooms. Unfortunately, the height of the floor levels, and the corresponding shallow soil coverage which accumulated over them after the Roman period, has meant that they have suffered very considerably from post-Roman agricultural activities, particularly the ploughing of the late Saxon and early Medieval periods. In many instances the floors and the concrete make-up beneath them have been scoured away by ploughing, which has carried the mutilated fragments, mixed with earth and building material, and deposited them in a thick layer of plough-derived soil in the lowlying area in front of the revetting wall. This continuous regrading activity has gradually led to the flattening out of the contours but it is, in itself, an interesting part of the history of the site and will be discussed in more detail in a later chapter (pp. 219-22). In spite of the destructive activity of the plough a remarkable amount of structural and decorative detail still survives.

Plate 22

The principal room in the wing lay exactly on the centre axis: it was a large square chamber 31 ft by 35 ft with an apsidal recess 20 ft in diameter opening out of its west wall. From its position and structure there can be little doubt that originally it served as an audience chamber, built in the style of the contemporary Italian examples, which its architect was so carefully trying to imitate. Almost the entire floor had been destroyed by ploughing, including much of the concrete and rubble beneath it, but a few small patches of a mosaic pavement survived; in the corner of the

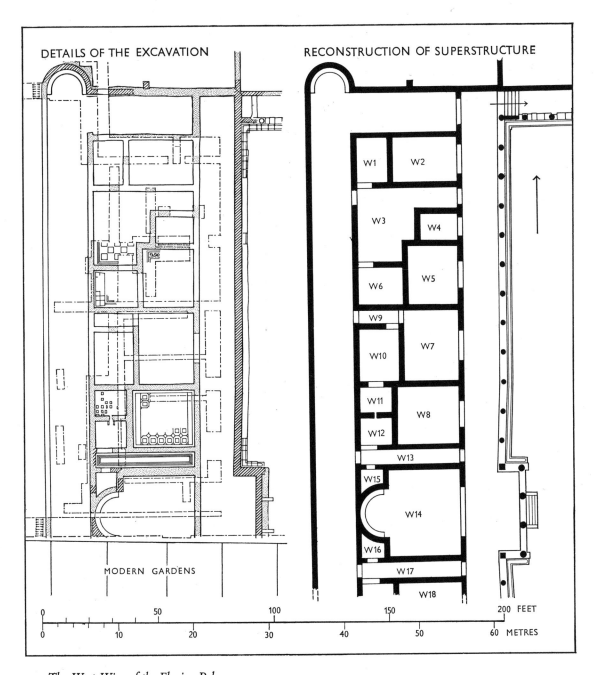

DETAILS OF THE EXCAVATION

RECONSTRUCTION OF SUPERSTRUCTURE

W1   W2
W3   W4
W6   W5
W9
W10 W7
W11 W8
W12
W13
W15
W14
W16
W17
W18

MODERN GARDENS

0   50   100   150   200 FEET
0   10   20   30   40   50   60 METRES

14   The West Wing of the Flavian Palace

apse an area showing a black border with a leaf inside it remained in position and further towards the centre of the room were two smaller areas
depicting a twisted guilloche design laid in white, black, yellow and red.

77

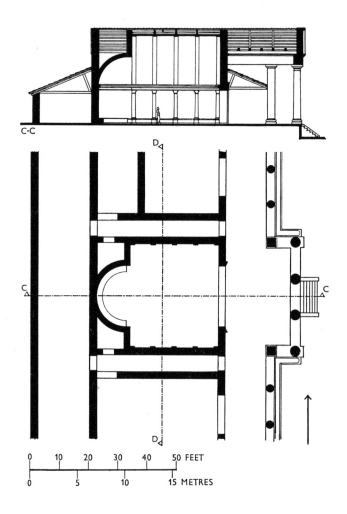

C-C

0 10 20 30 40 50 FEET

0 5 10 15 METRES

Fig. 15

The quality of the work was exceptionally fine with individual tesserae
$1/8$ to $3/10$ inch square laid very tightly and carefully together. Nowhere
in the rest of the Palace is there evidence of such exquisite craftsmanship.
The master mosaicist must have given the audience chamber his personal
attention.

The interior fittings of the room would have been largely moveable,
and of these there is no trace, but in the apse the impression made by a
timber bench was found lining the curved wall. In such a prominent
position, where the owner would have sat in state, we must imagine a
structure upholstered in high quality but nothing now survives apart
from its bare impression. We have, then, the ground plan of the room
and some traces of the interior layout, but it is also possible to reconstruct
the basic superstructure and to think of the room in terms of its volume

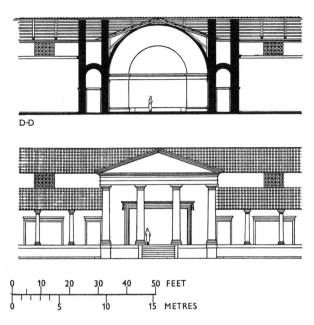

D-D

0   10   20   30   40   50 FEET

0   5   10   15 METRES

15, 16   Architectural reconstruction of the Audience Chamber

and carefully contrived visual effects. To begin with, the fronting colonnade gave way to a projecting platform in front of the room. This would have taken an impressive pedimented front supported on four large columns (the spacing of the columns elsewhere and the general proportions which can be deduced from them demand a tetrastyle treatment). The higher floor of the West Wing was reached, from the garden level, by a flight of wooden steps retained by sidewalls which exactly relate to the space between the two centre columns.

From the columns preserved in position in the north-west corner of the garden (p. 129), we know that the height of the veranda architrave would have been about 12 ft which, allowing for a sloping veranda roof and provision for windows above this in the main range to allow light into the rooms, would mean that the eaves of the range came at about 25 ft above the floor. Since this is almost exactly the height to which the four big columns supporting the pediment should have stood, the implication is that the audience chamber and the main range were roofed at the same height. These somewhat confusing calculations are much better expressed by the simple elevation reconstruction.

The most satisfactory way to have roofed the audience chamber would have been by means of a vault with its haunches resting on the north and

Fig. 16

0   5   10 *FEET*

0   1   2   3 *METRES*

17   *Flavian mosaic in room W 3 of the West Wing*

23 The mosaic pavement, of Flavian date, in the south-west corner of the North Wing (room N 4). Its design, picked out in black against a white background, was simply drawn in a style closely reminiscent of many contemporary Italian examples. In the third century the room was used as a workshop and the floor was allowed to wear out. When excavated it was found to be covered by masses of charred rafters and broken roof tiles from the final conflagration

24–26 The best preserved of the Flavian mosaic floors lay in the centre of the North Wing of the palace (room N 12). Its black and white design gives the impression of incomplete perspective. During the third period the room was divided by a timber partition which had been plastered and painted. Later the room was used for storage. *Opposite*, two of the details of the mosaic shown *above*. Part of the upper panel was subsequently, and inaccurately, patched

27 General view across the south-west corner of the North Wing showing the two first-century mosaics in what was later to be used as a workshop area

28 The first-century mosaic in room N13 was replaced by a polychrome floor about AD 100. The earlier floor can be seen in patches through holes in the later

29 One of the few coloured mosaics in the Flavian palace was found in room N 21 of the North Wing. The design was basically white against black but the large central squares were alternately red and blue. The small diamond shape on the left-hand side may have been the mosaicist's signature. The floor had slumped in places into the soft fillings of earlier features below

30, 31   The finest of the surviving coloured mosaics in the Flavian palace lay in room N 20 of the North Wing. The central circular panel is now missing, but around it was a band of alternating rosettes and vine-leaves enclosed by a twisted guilloche. The corners were filled by different motifs incorporating central vases with tendrils or fish on either side. A wide range of colours was used

32   The aisled hall lay in the corner between the North and East Wings. The main weight of its 70-ft span roof was taken on eight piers, the bases for which were massively constructed. The foundation of each was of flint set in concrete supporting a base of ashlar masonry and tiles. On this was placed a single large foundation block. The original floor would have been level with the base of the block. Towards the end of the first century additional bases were added, possibly to support statuary

33–35 In the East Wing of the palace lay a large colonnaded courtyard surrounded on three sides by a stylobate of limestone blocks, which originally supported the columns of the colonnade. In front of the stylobate was a ground-level gutter to collect rainwater (*opposite*). The gutter led to the north-east corner of the garden, where it opened into a culvert running beneath the veranda floor (*right*). In the second century the columns were pulled down and the old veranda was partitioned off and turned into a bath suite. *Above*, is shown part of the pillared hypocaust of the caldarium with the tesselated floor of the hot plunge bath beyond

36 The north-west corner of the main formal garden of the palace, showing the stylobate and gutter fronting the veranda with fragments of the columns lying where they had fallen. In the corner is the masonry foundation for a water-tank

37 View across the centre of the formal garden, showing the bedding trenches for hedges cut in- >
to the gravel. The pond in the centre of the trench is modern (see Plate II)

38 The north-west corner of the formal garden of the Flavian palace. The modern building (background) is constructed exactly upon the walls of the Roman North Wing. In front is a veranda and stylobate with three column-bases still in position. At the west (left-hand) side the stylobate abuts the revetting wall in front of the West Wing. The ground-level gutter is well preserved in this section. The narrow trenches, some of them now water-filled, are the bedding trenches for shrubs or bushes flanking the pathways. A length of ceramic water pipe can be seen along the west side of the west path

39 The north-east corner of the formal garden, looking south. In the fore-ground is the robber trench for the gutter which once flanked the northern colonnade. The bedding trenches can be clearly seen, delineating the edges of the paths. Two lengths of water-pipe are visible, the curved stretch originally ran unhindered from the water-tower in the north-west corner of the garden to the area south of the central path, the straighter length served fountains arranged around the northern paths

40 One of the column capitals found in the East Wing of the palace; columns of this type, 11–12 ft high, would have stood at 11-ft intervals around the gardens of the palace. Some of the stone from which they were made came from Gloucestershire, some from France

41, 42 *Above*, a Roman wall-painting of a garden adorn- > ing the so-called 'garden room' of Livia from the Prima Porta, north of Rome. The painting depicts a typical formal garden with neat pathways divided by recessed fences from areas of densely planted vegetation. At Fishbourne the same arrangement was adopted, but instead of fences the paths were lined by hedges planted in loam-filled bedding trenches. The recess shown here (*below*) contains a single bedding pit, presumably for a tree, a very similar feature to that shown above

43   In front of the audience chamber the revetting wall, which retained the higher platform of the
West Wing, was brought forward to form a porch area reached by a flight of steps. The wall was
of flint and mortar faced with limestone blocks and rendered with mortar. At ground-level were
the massive blocks of the gutter

south walls. Such an arrangement would have focussed attention on the apsidal recess, itself roofed with a semi-dome, and at the same time it would have created feelings of space which a flat ceiling would not. An examination of the wall footings showed that the north wall, which would have been about 2 ft thick, stood on a wide footing about 5 ft across. This is quite exceptional in the Palace and implies that this wall, and presumably the south wall which was not available for excavation, supported a considerable weight, the thrusts of which it was necessary to dissipate with the extra footing width. The structural evidence is therefore strongly in favour of these walls supporting a vaulted ceiling. Such a construction would not necessarily have been very heavy, frequently they were built of timber and stucco, but even so the stresses, particularly the lateral thrusts, would have required footings of some strength. Additional evidence for the vaulted ceiling is provided by the recovery of a number of fragments of stucco from the room showing raised ribs picked out in white against a background of bright blue, purple and red. Some of the pieces have a slight curve, strongly suggesting that they came from a vault. Therefore, using the few scraps of surviving evidence together with a consideration of the general principles of Roman architecture, it is possible to reconstruct the general form of the room and an impression of what it may have looked like inside. The details of decoration are, of course, unsupported by firm evidence but the general volume and proportions shown must be close to the original.

Audience chambers of this kind are fairly well known in the Mediterranean world, the closest near contemporary example being in the famous palace of Domitian on the Palatine in Rome.[22] It has been suggested that the huge soaring vault of the roof and the semi-domed recess in which the Emperor would have sat in state are an attempt to capture in masonry the feeling of a god sitting in heaven. It is perhaps significant that the idea of the apsidal ended audience chamber seems to have been behind the earliest forms of Christian church!

The Fishbourne audience chamber lay in the centre of a long range of rooms but it was divided from them by flanking corridors which served as a convenient means of access from one side of the building to the other, and at the same time helped to isolate the room from the noise of the rest of the building. The rooms to the north seem to have been planned as two blocks, numbers W 1–6 forming one and W 7–12 the other. In the northern block room W 3 served as a general concourse from which access to the other rooms was probably provided, but only one doorway

Fig. 17
Plate 16

leading to room W 6 has survived the extensive destruction. All of the rooms were originally floored with black and white mosaic pavements but those in rooms W 1, 2, and 4 have been almost totally destroyed. In room W 3, however, a substantial area survives of a complex pattern of square panels linked with areas of a Greek key pattern which also spread into the areas between the panels. The panels are filled with a wide variety of geometric motifs. This general type of arrangement was very popular in Italy in the first century AD and can be paralleled on many of the early sites in Rome and at Herculaneum and Pompeii. The same type of pattern was used again at Fishbourne in room N 13 in the centre of the North Wing.

Plate 15

The mosaic in room W 6 incorporated totally different ideas. It was divided into two parts: a 'mat' of chequer pattern along the west wall and the main 'carpet' filling the rest of the room. The division was made so that a person entering through the door in the north-west corner would walk out onto the mat and would be able to obtain a clear view of the entire carpet. Sadly, very little of the carpet area has survived except for its border of black triangles arranged base to apex, but there may have been a figured design in the centre – we will never know. Of the mosaic in room W 5 only a small corner now remains showing a bordering panel of tendrils, about 2 ft wide, which would have run the full length of the room, possibly balanced by a similar panel on the opposite side of the room, as was the case with room W 8. Although the floor was largely a black-on-white design, the node of the tendril which survived was picked out in yellow. If the simple arrangement here was like that in room W 8, then the nodes would have alternated red and yellow.

The cold all-over black and white of the floors contrasted sharply with the rich bright colours with which the walls were painted. From the surviving pieces of wall plaster it appears that the walls of room W 3 were painted as an area of composite mock marble inlay, one of a blue-grey colour given a vague texture by smearing with a wide brush, another next to it was basically purple deliberately splashed with red and white to give a speckled appearance. These two areas were divided from each other by black and white lines meant to represent a simple moulding. These 'marble sheets' probably formed the dado above which would have been areas painted in plain bright colours. Evidence of the decor of room W 6 also survived. Here there were areas of pink over-painted with bold purple designs together with areas of red, pale blue and purple.

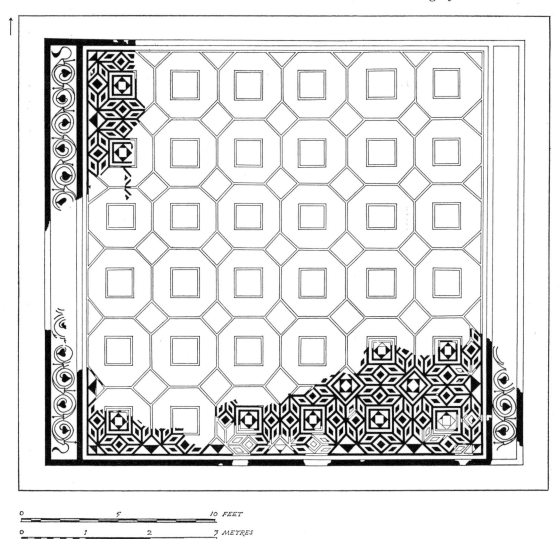

0   5   10 *FEET*

0   1   2   3 *METRES*

18   Flavian mosaic in room W 8 of the West Wing

The second set of rooms, numbers W 7–12, were rather differently arranged: two big rooms, W 7 and 8, fronted directly onto the veranda
and were entered through wide east-facing doorways. These were clearly
important state apartments second only to the audience chamber. Behind
them were four other rooms, all floored with pink mortar. Room W 9
served as a corridor leading from W 7 to the back of the building and
incidentally giving access to room W 10 through various doors, the

timber sills of two of which have survived. Room W 10 was a simple unadorned room out of which opened the smaller W 11, the floor of which was heated by a hypocaust, the only example of central heating in the Flavian Palace outside the bath block. The stoking chamber for the hypocaust was provided in room W 12, which could be entered only from the corridor to the south. This back range with its heated room is an interesting feature, but not immediately easy to explain. One possibility, however, is that the rooms formed a suite to which guests might retire during a chilly evening: the front rooms would have caught the sun all day but the west-facing side would have benefited only from the weaker evening sun – perhaps some booster heat was required.

Plates 17, 18
Fig. 18

Rooms W 7 and 8 were probably both floored with mosaics, but the floor of room W 7 has been totally destroyed. In W 8, however, substantial areas of mosaic work remain. The main design, in black and white, was a highly repetitive arrangement of the box-within-box pattern which was so popular in the Roman world. On either side of it were long tendril panels drawn in black, yellow and red, on a white background. The relatively dull all-over pattern would have been acceptable in a room frequently used and perhaps partly obscured by furniture. Unlike the floor in W 6 it was not constructed to impress visitors.

Plate 21

The room with the heated floor, room W 11, produced sufficient painted wall plaster to show that its walls were rendered with pink mortar which was painted in areas of plain red and plain white adjacent to each other, with the junction between the colours overpainted with a thin black line. The red probably came from the dado while the wall above was simply painted white. It seems that somewhere in the room, just below the ceiling, over the door or perhaps framing a window or recess, an elaborate cornice had been painted and elsewhere in the decor there were areas of bright blue-green.

Plate 20

The two small alcoves behind the audience chamber were floored with white mortar: they were probably nothing more than store rooms leading out of the flanking corridors. But the north corridor at least was an essential part of the stylish range, for it was floored with a very simple

Plate 19

black and white mosaic in which the central white panel was carefully constructed of tesserae laid diagonally to the borders.

Of the plan of the rest of the wing south of the audience chamber we are completely ignorant. The land now lies beneath modern houses and gardens and is not available for excavation, but it was in this area that two school children, digging in 1938, discovered a well preserved piece of black and white mosaic pavement. Their discovery holds out the hope that one day it may be possible to examine the rest of the wing.

As the plan shows, the main range of rooms was surrounded by wide verandas and, as we have suggested, the east veranda was colonnaded so that the rooms facing east had a clear view of the garden. The problem of the colonnades will be considered separately in the next chapter. How the western corridor was treated is much less clear: in plan it was 17 ft wide and ran the entire length of the wing, finishing at its north end, and presumably also the south, with a large apsidal recess lined originally with a stone-built bench. This much is clear but its width is excessive for a simple service corridor and unlike the east-facing veranda with its colonnade forming an important visual part of the great garden, there is no reason to suppose the existence of a west-facing colonnade, nor is there any evidence for gardens to the west requiring a colonnade of this kind. One explanation, however, might be that the corridor served as an exercise space, a *hippodromos*, in which one might play games or run from end to end pausing to rest in the alcoves. A closely similar arrangement is known in Domitian's palace[23] and is by no means uncommon in other early Roman villas in Italy. If this were so, the west wall might have been perforated with large windows or even provided with balustrades so that the evening light could reach the interior.

The corridor was decorated in the same style throughout with a dado of pink splashed with black, white and ochre to imitate a coarse-grained marble: at the base of the dado was a narrow deep red skirting. The main walls above the dado level were painted white marked out in panels bordered by deep red bands, and concentric with the red borders were thin black frame lines. The apse was picked out for a more specialized treatment. Here the wall panels were yellow with a thin brown frame line. The colours were deliberately kept simple and light as would befit an area set aside for gentle exercise and relaxation.

From the foregoing description it would appear that the West Wing was laid out to dominate the great garden which lay in front of it. With its central pedimented front supported on four large columns and reached by a flight of steps, it was designed to impress but at the same time it was essentially an extension of the garden environment – a visitor walking in the garden had direct access to all its main rooms. This 'semi-public' aspect of the plan only underlines the idea that the audience chamber and the flanking state rooms were the administrative and official rooms. As we shall see, the other wings were conceived in a totally different way.

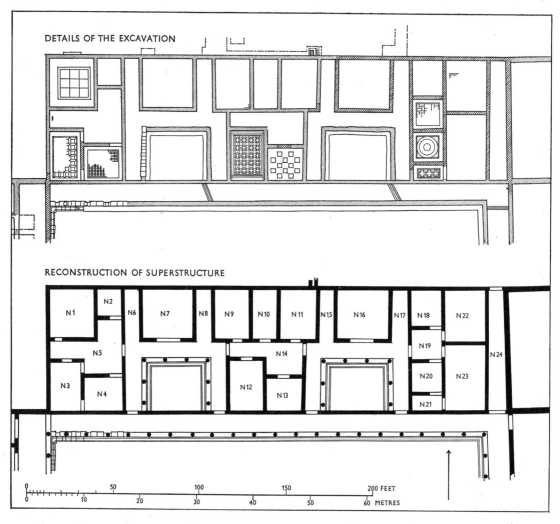

DETAILS OF THE EXCAVATION

RECONSTRUCTION OF SUPERSTRUCTURE

19 *The North Wing of the Flavian Palace*

The North Wing

Fig. 19

The North Wing lay in a single block, measuring some 70 ft by 255 ft, across the north side of the garden. Its 23 rooms were arranged rather like a letter E, the spaces between the short arms being occupied by small private gardens surrounded on three sides by colonnades and closed on the fourth with a blank wall. The whole wing seems to have been designed as a group of two or three private suites turned in upon their own gardens to provide luxury and peace. The first suite, comprising rooms N 1–5, is not unlike the northern part of the West Wing in plan. It is essentially four rooms opening out of a general concourse (N 5) which seems to have been floored with a simple black and white mosaic. Room N 1, the largest in the suite, was provided with a complex mosaic floor, a small part of which now survives showing it to consist of a rigid geometric pattern of squares-within-squares picked out in black with the limited use of red and blue.

Fig. 20

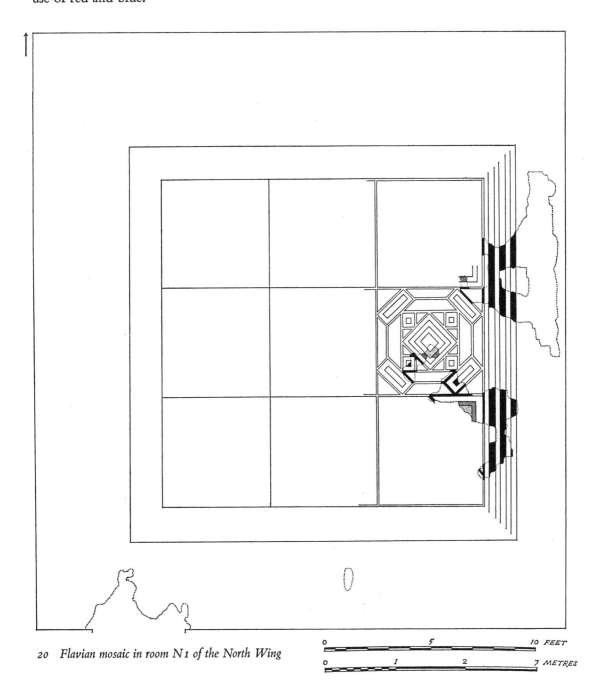

20 *Flavian mosaic in room N1 of the North Wing*

21   *Flavian mosaic in room N3 of the North Wing*

Room N2 had been so altered in later times that nothing of the original
Flavian decoration survived but the floors of rooms N3 and 4 remained
virtually intact, apart from some holes which were allowed to wear in
them when the rooms were later given over to domestic functions.
The position of the original door sills show that, in addition to being
entered direct from the concourse, they were interlinked by a door which
at a later stage was walled up. The mosaic floor in room N3 was a
relatively simple arrangement of square panels, linked together by a dia-
mond-patterned border, and filled with one of three geometric motifs.

Fig. 21
Plate 26

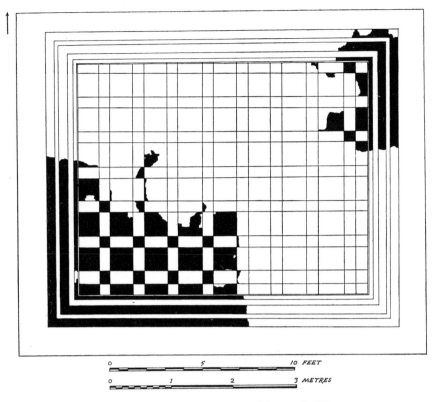

22 *Flavian mosaic in room N4 of the North Wing*

Plate 27
Fig. 22

The basic feeling was one of lightness and simplicity. In contrast the floor in room N4 consisted of a repetitive arrangement of black squares of two sizes on a white ground; here the impression is of darkness. The floors, of course, are only one part of the decorative design; to fully appreciate their effect it would be necessary to see them in relation to the wall and ceiling painting but unfortunately, in the case of rooms N3 and 4 nothing of the original painting scheme survives.

Between the western suite and the central suite lay the simple colon-naded courtyard with a single large room, N7, fronting on to it. The room was flanked by two elongated rooms or corridors, rooms N6 and 8, both of which had been subjected to considerable later alteration leaving their original function far from clear. While it is not totally impossible that they served as stairways to an upper storey, there is no other evidence to suggest more than one floor and moreover four stairways (rooms N6, 8, 15 and 17) would seem a little excessive. A more likely explanation is that they were used as service rooms in connection with dining, for which room N7 and its counterpart room N16 are so well designed. Little is known of the interior decoration of room N7. It had originally been provided with a mosaic pavement but only a row or two of the edge tesserae now survive in position, the rest of the pavement having been removed before the second-century floor was laid. The mass of wall plaster recovered from the rubble filling the room is more likely to belong to the second-century phase of alterations and will accordingly be described later. From the north robber trench, however, came several pieces of two stucco mouldings which almost certainly belong to the original Flavian decor. The best preserved depicts a simple frieze of pairs of birds holding fruit in their beaks and standing on either side of a vase of fruit.

Fig. 23
Plate 70

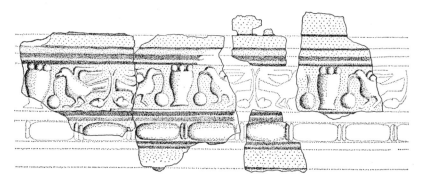

23   *Fragments of a stucco moulding found in the North Wing, length 20 cms*

Sufficient survives to show that the design is repetitive and a careful examination of the join between one section and the next clearly demonstrates how each section was impressed onto the damp plaster, presumably with a wooden block. The simple cornice moulding above the frieze and the bead-and-reel below were probably applied in this way. It is not difficult to imagine the feelings of boredom which the plasterer must have experienced faced with enormous expanses of moulding, all to be carefully tooled and stamped in this mechanical fashion.

The 'bird moulding' was of sufficient proportions to have occupied the junction between wall and ceiling, but the second moulding, a small section simply decorated in what is known as an egg-and-dart motif, probably comes from lower down on the walls, framing perhaps a recess set into a wall face. The discovery of moulded stucco is remarkable in Britain. It was a technique common enough in Rome but for some reason it did not seem to find favour in this country. Moulded stucco, of a rather different kind, has been found on only one other site, a villa on the outskirts of Verulamium (St Albans). While more will, no doubt, eventually be found, stucco work can never have been popular in Roman Britain.

A considerable quantity of early wall plaster was recovered from the courtyard, coming from the faces of the walls which formed its west, north and east sides. The west wall and part at least of the north wall were painted with a pink and purple background which served as a basis for bold green and blue foliage painting. The east wall was, however, more restrained with a dado of painted mock marble slabs in varying tones of splashed and smeared purple and green, each divided from the next by simply painted vertical 'mouldings'. Above the dado came a band of red merging to yellow representing a simple cornice moulding, with bands of deep blue, bright green and red above. An exactly similar type of painting was also recovered from the north-west corner of the courtyard.

The central suite, rooms N 9–13, was arranged around the L-shaped room N 14 which formed a concourse as well as allowing free access between the two courtyards. Out of it must have opened doors leading to the five adjacent rooms. Traces of the original floor show that it was of mosaic with, in one area at least, the tesserae set in rows diagonally to the borders in the style of corridor W 13. The black and white mosaic which now occupies the southern part of the room, though laid in the style of the early floors, can be shown to overlie part of the original mosaic and is therefore later. It may be, however, that in its present form it is simply a relaid version of the original using the same materials and copying the same design but with less craftsmanship. Alternatively it may be a copy of the early mosaic in room N 12. At any event it is interesting that the later occupiers should want to retain the style of the Flavian decor.

A small area of wall plaster survived in position in the south-west corner of the room. It belonged to the dado which here was painted pink and splashed with blue and red with the joints between the marbled areas shown as a simple black line. Only 9 ins survived of the dado which would originally have been about 3 ft high, but indications of the wall panels above are provided by fragments lying loose in the rubble, including areas painted in plain green, yellow, orange, red and blue with interior frame lines very much in the style of the wall painting of the proto-palace.

The three rooms which form the northern part of the middle suite (N 9–11) were all refloored in the later period after most of the original mosaics had been ripped up. Now all that remains of the original floors is a few of the tesserae around the edges of the rooms and a small patch of mosaic in the south-east corner of room N9, comparable in style to the 'mat' already described in room W6 in the West Wing. The importance of these rooms lies in the remarkable state of preservation of the wall decoration, which probably dates back to the Flavian period. Room N9 yielded a large quantity of painted wall plaster, much of it in quite large pieces allowing a fairly full reconstruction of the design. Here, more than anywhere else in the Palace, it is possible to appreciate the rich, almost overbearing, nature of the mock marble painting. Like most of the first-century designs the room was provided with a dado about 3 ft high painted in imitation of large sheets of boldly veined pink and red marble, each 'sheet' divided from the next by a vertical black line intended to represent the junction between the individual slabs. Above this was an elaborate horizontal cornice painted in stripes of black and white, to represent highlight and shadow, and a green merging to orange which resembles a gently curving moulding. Above the cornice the wall was divided into a series of rectangular panels capped by another cornice a foot or more below the ceiling height. The panels were of two types, the very elaborate representation of multicoloured inlaid marble and much simpler areas of speckled orange, or speckled deep blue to contrast with them and relieve their vividness. One of the multicoloured panels has been reconstructed from the fragments: it shows a central slab of blue-green and green veined marble as though a single sheet had been split through the middle and opened out, the two halves being placed side by side. This centrepiece was surrounded by a highly complex frame composed of painted mouldings and fillets of varying coloured marbles. A simple verbal description makes the decor sound tasteless and oppressive but it must be remembered that these elaborately painted walls belonged to very large rooms (room N9 was 20 ft by 29 ft) floored with plain black and white mosaics. In these circumstances carefully controlled marble-style painting with a correct balance between the multi-coloured and plain panels could well have been visually very exciting, though perhaps more in tune with Victorian sensibilities than with those of today.

While most of the rooms were painted to represent marble inlay one at least, room N7, was inlaid with real marble in a large panel or series of panels which remained in position until the Palace was finally destroyed 200 years later, when the slabs peeled off the wall and fell in heaps onto the floor. A wide range of marble was employed including the local

British Purbeck marble (a blue highly fossiliferous limestone) and a grey siltstone probably also from the Isle of Purbeck. The imported marbles include white crystalline marble from Turkey, a green and white veined marble from the Pyrenees, a yellow and white marble from the Haute-Garrone and at least two types from Greece including one from the island of Skyros. The interior designers of the Palace clearly had a wide range of the most exotic veneers available to them – no expense was spared. Although the panel had fallen from the wall it was possible to see that some of the pieces still lay in the positions relative to each other that they had occupied *in situ*, for example a triangle of green veined Pyrenean marble was bordered by two fillets of white Turkish marble which in turn were enclosed by strips of grey-brown siltstone, arranged so as to give the maximum contrast between the high quality shiny marble and the draber local material. All kinds of shapes were found in such confusion that reconstruction was impossible, but it looks as though the design included arrangements of squares set diagonally within squares as well as octagons, or pentagons, placed within circles. Arrangements of this kind are well known on the continent, particularly at Herculaneum.

Room N 10 also provided evidence for the use of marble mouldings carved from white Turkish marble and blue Purbeck marble, several of which lay scattered in the rubble on its floor. Others were recovered from elsewhere in the building. The Purbeck mouldings tended to be heavier than those carved from the Turkish marble, suggesting that they served as the vertical members framing doorways or recesses, while the lighter Turkish mouldings were used as horizontal cornices across the top. This view is supported by an examination of the methods of attachment of the two types, the Purbeck mouldings were simply mortared in position, which would be an acceptable method for verticals, whilst the Turkish mouldings showed signs of being clamped to the wall with small iron hooks, a type of firmer attachment which would have been essential if they were displayed in a horizontal position. In addition to framing mouldings, marble slabs carved in a variety of other ways have been found, several of the pieces belonging to large moulded panels while one unique piece of Purbeck marble was carved on its upper surface with somewhat stylized leaves. Apart from saying that it was evidently part of a large and important panel there is no indication of its form or original position.

The two rooms on the south side of the concourse both retained substantial areas of their original mosaic floors. In room N 13 several square

Plate 28

Plates 23–25

Fig. 24

feet of the black and white Flavian mosaic can be seen through a hole in the later floor which seals it. Although the early mosaic had been partly destroyed before the upper one was laid, probably to provide raw materials for it, much of the original design still survives, showing it to have incorporated areas of Greek key patterns. The floor next door in room N 12 is much better preserved because the room was at no subsequent period refloored; instead it was divided by a timber partition and the original mosaic allowed to serve for 200 years as the floor of both rooms. The pattern is an interesting combination of motifs and arrangements which recur on first-century floors on the continent: it is simply a series of cross motifs, variously patterned, arranged between square panels some containing squares-diagonally-within-squares, others stylized compass-drawn rosettes, and others fleurs-de-lis. The crosses and boxes are linked together with a square and diamond background. Both ends of the floor are provided with strips of simpler patterns to help the design fit into the shape of the room. The arrangement is by no means as dull as the verbal description suggests, all the elements are carefully contrived to give the maximum visual effect – an impression of perspective, but an incomplete perspective so that the eye is confused: at one time a square might appear to stand out as a cube – but never completely, it is pulled back into reverse by some other part of the design so that the whole floor appears to move and flicker. The care with which the floor was later patched, even if skill was lacking, and the fact that it was retained for so long in the divided room might suggest that it remained a popular feature for some time.

The walls of room N 12 had been elaborately painted in the Flavian period and had been allowed to remain untouched even after the partition was inserted. The dado, parts of which could be reconstructed to a height of 22 ins, was pink splashed with deep red to look rather like an expensive granite and above this would have been panels painted to resemble even more exotic stones: deep red splashed with black and white, yellow painted with sinuous red veins, speckled deep blue and green and areas of greyish-white with red veins. Like the arrangement in room N9 these richly textured areas were enclosed by strips and fillets of other 'marbles' to make up highly ornate panels relieved with intervening areas of plain red and deep blue. While the basic arrangements in rooms N9 and 12 were very close, the marbling was different. The painters must have had an enormous repertoire as well as a desire that no two rooms should look the same. Yet another composition was adopted in room

24   *Flavian mosaic in room N 12 of the North Wing. The dotted line marks the limit of a later patch*

N 13 where the dado was of orange-red splashed with green with areas of plain red and finely painted marbling above.

Nowhere at Fishbourne is there any firm evidence of furniture or fittings, nor should any be expected to survive the 200 years of use and subsequent destruction, but some hints of the positions of furniture may be given by the arrangements of the mosaics. Those with overall patterns

113

I   Mid-second-century mosaic in room N7 of the North Wing, showing the central panel of the floor

II   General view of the north side of the path running across the centre of the former garden. The bedding trenches, which once contained marled loam to support bushes, can be clearly seen

I

would not be spoilt by thoughtless placing, but in the case of room W6 with its 'mat and carpet' it is clear that certain areas were meant to be looked at. In room N13 a patch of burning on the original mosaic hints at the use of braziers to provide warmth during long winter evenings. The architect, presumably unused to designing for the British climate, had omitted to provide central heating. Braziers were a commonly used but less satisfactory alternative. Room N12 also shows signs of discolouration by fire but unlike room N13, where the early mosaic was sealed by a later floor, the mosaic in room N12 was in use at the time of the final conflagration. In this case burning rafters are a more likely cause.

East of the central suite lay a second colonnaded garden overlooked by a large room, N16, the equivalent of N7 to the west. This part of the building had suffered considerably from subsidence and from deliberate dismantling long before the final destruction and, in consequence, very little other than foundations survives. Part of one of the columns from the courtyard lay in the general rubble and from the garden area came a small fragment of painted wall plaster depicting a fluted urn from a garden scene, presumably once painted on the wall backing the colonnade. It is an interesting reminder that not all the walls simulated marble inlay. As we shall see later some of the freer painting is of extremely high quality.

The eastern suite of the North Wing, rooms N18–23, contained some of the finest mosaics to survive in the Palace. The general arrangement of the rooms differs from the other two North Wing suites in that there is no obvious concourse, but the plan would demand that room N19 served as a general way through to rooms N10, 22 and 23 beyond, and it could well have been linked with rooms N18 and 20. The room itself was floored with a basically white mosaic simply picked out with a black geometric design. Immediately next door in room N20 was an altogether more impressive mosaic, one of the very few truly polychrome floors to be found in the Palace, consisting of a central circular design set within a square. The circle was composed of a twisted rope-like guilloche in a wide range of colours on a black background within which came a circular band of rosettes alternating with heart-shaped leaves both drawn in red, yellow and white, outlined in black and shown against a white background. The central circular area which lay within has unfortunately been totally destroyed, but in such a position one might have expected a finely figured centrepiece. Some idea of the quality of the mosaicist's figure drawing comes out in the designs which he fitted into the spandrels be-

Plates 30, 31
Plate VII

tween the circular framing panels and the border of the square. Each corner was different, one had two dolphins facing a vase, another was similar but with fish instead of dolphins, whilst the remaining two contained urns with high square-topped handles and tendrils growing from their bases. All four were very skilfully drawn and carefully designed to fit the difficult triangular spaces available.

Mosaics of this kind, unknown elsewhere in Britain, are rare even in Italy but the basic arrangement of a large circular panel set within a square recurs on several of the Italian sites. What is a little less usual is the use of the complicated guilloche to enclose the centre circle. Its layout and successful execution required considerable skill and experience.

Plate 29

Room N21 probably served as an anteroom to N20. With its simple mosaic of black overlaid by large squares of red and blue enlivened by interlocking white frames, it would have made a striking contrast to the more delicate floral floor next door. It is difficult to believe that the juxtaposition of these two was not deliberately contrived to make a dramatic visual impact on an unsuspecting visitor. One interesting detail survives on the border of the floor where a small diamond shape made from white tesserae is set into the black surround. Since it is so evidently not part of the design it may have been the signature of the mosaicist.

The floors of the remaining three rooms do not survive to any extent except for small patches of a simple black and white mosaic in room N22. Roman destruction and recent ploughing has removed everything else. It is a great pity that some trace of the wall decoration in rooms N20 and 21 has not survived. It would have been interesting to have seen how the designers tackled the problem posed by small rooms with multi-coloured floors, for they could hardly have used the heavy style of marbling commonly employed elsewhere in rooms with simple black and white floors. A second, totally different, style is, however, known from a mass of painted wall plaster, which at some stage had been carried out of the North Wing and dumped in a hollow immediately to the west. It may have been removed when redecorating was being carried out early in the second century, or alternatively when the east end of the wing was demolished a little later. At any event its original position cannot now be recovered. The quality of the work is extremely fine. Basically the walls were painted yellow and upon this even background two types of isolated panels were drawn, one in various tones of plain untextured red representing recesses, the edges carefully shaded and the corners mitred to give the impression of depth, the others were scenes which might have appeared as distant views seen through windows. Between the recesses and scenes the yellow walls were enlivened with simple foliage in green and brown with exquisitely painted rose-buds.

One fragment showing the corner of a scene is of particular signifi- Plate VI
cance. The picture, painted with a restricted colour range of blue, brown and white, shows part of the front elevation of a colonnaded building with the sea in the background. It is brilliantly executed with simple brush strokes recapturing the quality of a choppy sea and sunlit building, but what is even more important is that an almost identical painting is known at Stabiae, one of the towns to suffer during the eruption of Ve- suvius in AD 79. The same colour range, similar subject matter (a harbour scene at Stabiae) and an identical, almost impressionistic, style of brush- work strongly suggests that the two paintings were carried out by the same school of artists if not by the same man. This one small fragment is perhaps the most dramatic link of all between Flavian Fishbourne and the contemporary metropolitan world.

The superstructure of the North Wing is relatively easy to reconstruct in outline. The verandas of the gardens would have had inward sloping roofs above which the walls of the rooms would have towered so that clear-storey light could have been provided. In all probability the three main blocks were roofed with north-south pitched roofs ending on three imposing gables overlooking the great garden. East-west roofs of lower pitch would have been sufficient to cover the rest. The only means of access needed would have been two doors opening from the southern- fronting colonnade into the peristyles of the two private gardens. Such an arrangement would have afforded the maximum amount of peace for the residents.

It will be seen from the above description that the North Wing was planned and built on a grand scale with private colonnaded gardens, suites of spacious rooms and elaborate interior decoration. There can be little doubt that it was designed as a residential wing to provide luxurious accommodation – possibly for visitors. The plan would have allowed it to have been used as at least three separate suites.

The South Wing

The discovery and reconstruction of the South Wing was in many ways one of the most satisfying parts of the entire excavation, partly because it was unexpected but largely because with a minimum expenditure of

energy one of the major problems of the site was suddenly and con-
clusively overcome. It had been realized for some years after the beginning of the excavation that the south side of the 'great courtyard' defined
by the East, North and West Wings was closed in some way either by a
range of rooms, a plain wall or, more likely we thought, by a simple
colonnaded walk to allow a view from the garden south to the sea. It
was not until the summer of 1967, the last major season, that a chance arose
to examine the problem when the owners of a house on the south side of
the main road invited us to excavate in their garden. One of the first
trenches cut in the courtyard behind the house revealed the footings for
a stylobate, which once supported a colonnade, and the trench where the
ground-level gutter had been immediately in front of it. The discovery
was not particularly spectacular but in terms of the ground plan it is of
vital importance, for it showed not only that a major range of rooms
existed across the south but that it was provided with a south-facing view
worthy of a colonnade. A few further trial trenches dug in the front
garden confirmed the existence of the range and allowed two of the cross
walls to be planned. In the following year details of the east end of the
wing were examined in the front garden of another house.

Using these small fragments of ground plan in conjunction with what
is known of the rest of the Palace allowed the general shape of the wing
to be reconstructed, for the south side is known and the north side can be
fixed, supposing that it was symmetrically sited in relation to the central
east-west axis which passed through the audience chamber. Similarly the
east end has been defined by excavation, while the west probably lay in
the same relationship to the West Wing, as does the end of the North
Wing. Based on these calculations the range of rooms would be some
52 ft wide by 272 ft long with colonnades on both the north and south
sides – a remarkable return in information for the effort expanded on so
few trial trenches. There are, of course, a number of details that need
checking and we know little of the internal arrangement of the rooms
but at present no more land is available for excavation, nor is most of
the area ever likely to become so.

One interesting problem to be raised is how much of the Flavian South
Wing derived from the South Wing of the Neronian proto-palace and
how much was built onto it in the Flavian period. The structures examined in the centre of the wing are constructed in the style of the
Flavian work, but those at the extreme east end are clearly part of the
earlier building which had simply been incorporated into the new Palace.

The junction lies somewhere between and is not yet available for study.

Little can be said of the interior decoration of this South Wing largely because of the intensive robbing to which the area has been subjected, as well as the destructive effects of road building and the construction of the houses, but it must have been in this area that the black and white mosaic pavement, 13 $^1/_2$ ft wide, was found when the road was widened in 1805. The excavations have also produced loose tesserae and pieces of painted wall plaster, leaving little doubt that the wing was finely adorned.

The nature of the superstructure depends upon the internal arrangement of the rooms which at present is ill known (one good sewer trench along the south side of the A27, however, would solve most of the uncertainties). The simplest reconstruction would be to suppose that the range was roofed beneath a single continuous roof with gables at each end, but such an arrangement while functionally adequate would have been visually so dull that the monotony must have been relieved with cross ridges and other elaborations to break up the single sweep.

That the wing faced south across a private garden, which we will see was elaborately landscaped, strongly suggests that it was a residential range of some significance, quite possibly the private residence of the owner. If this is accepted it will explain one difficulty which had hitherto remained – the siting of the bath suite in the extreme south-east corner of the Palace. All the time that the North Wing was thought to be the owner's residence it was puzzling why the bath suite should be so far away, nearly five minutes walk on a wet night. The discovery of the South Wing and its tentative identification as the owner's suite neatly overcomes the problem, for the baths were now conveniently close, at the end of the corridor.

The East Wing

The East Wing, nearly 500 ft long, was an amalgam of several different architectural features strung out and given visual unity by a colonnade facing into the garden and an impressive monumental east front – the face which the Palace presented to the outside world. In the centre lay the entrance hall, the visual and functional axis of the wing, while in the far north-east corner was a great aisled hall also provided with an imposing façade. Between them lay two colonnaded gardens flanked by a single range of rooms. The arrangement south of the entrance hall is altogether more confused, partly by the superincumbant modern buildings and

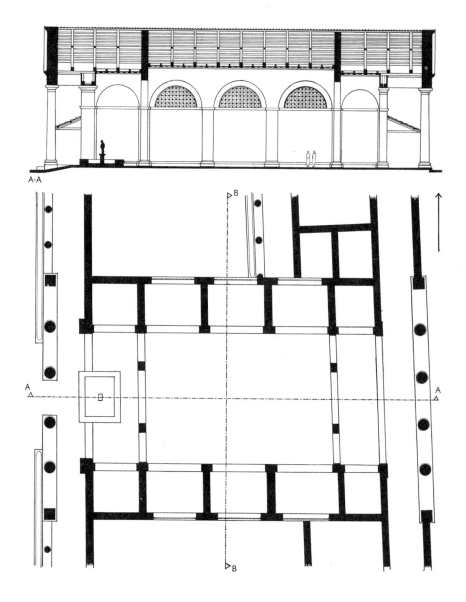

partly because of the integration of the earlier proto-palace into the new design. The general impression gained is that a certain symmetry was arrived at by regarding the peristyle of the proto-palace, and a rather awkward wedge-shaped space created between it and the entrance hall, as equivalent to the two courtyards on the north side and incorporating the rooms of the proto-palace into a range again reflecting a similar arrangement to the north. To complete the balance a monumental façade would have been needed to front the bath suite, but the area has not been extensively examined and no positive evidence for this has yet come to light.

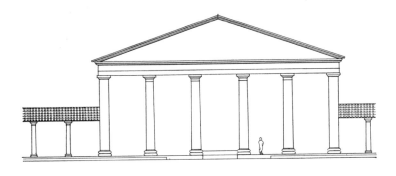

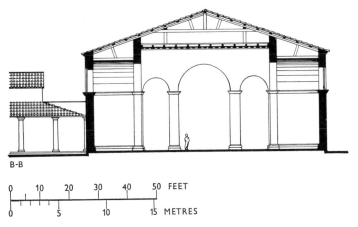

25, 26   Architectural reconstruction of the Entrance Hall in the East Wing

It was the entrance hall that was meant to impress the most, for through here all visitors had to pass. It is hardly surprising, therefore, that it was designed as the largest room in the entire Palace, 80 ft wide by 105 ft long. It was provided at its east and west fronts with enormous pedimented façades, each supported on six large columns standing to a height of about 26 ft – this much is suggested by the widening of the footings in front of the hall, the interior arrangement of the walls and the general proportions of the colonnades elsewhere in the Palace. Internally the room consisted of the main hall with a series of small rooms or cubicles opening out of each side. This arrangement was partly structural, so as to provide additional lateral support across the enormous distance which would otherwise have had to be roofed, and partly for visual effect, to create interesting spaces only incompletely seen from any one position so that a visitor would have been encouraged to move on to examine them. Incomplete vistas of this kind were frequently employed by Roman

Fig. 25

Fig. 26

architects, particularly when there was a need to create a flow of people to prevent congestion. In terms of the superstructure at Fishbourne it is probable that the 'cubicles' were spaced behind continuous side arcades, the arcade walls thus reducing the greatest span of the area to 49 ft, which was quite manageable as far as availability of timber for ceiling and rafters was concerned. As the reconstruction suggests, the alcoves were probably provided with lower ceilings than the main hall, but high enough to allow large lunettes to be placed in the side walls. Lunettes in this position would have been essential to allow light into the hall and the brightly lit alcoves themselves opening from behind arcades would have provided attractive settings for statuary.

Two footings were discovered running across the hall, dividing off bays at each end. The western footing was sufficiently well preserved to show that for most of its length it was a 'sleeper wall', i.e. a below floor level footing, which supported two rectangular pier bases evenly placed on either side of the central axis. These bases show beyond doubt that the hall was divided at this point by a screen wall composed of a large central arch flanked by two narrower, and therefore correspondingly lower, side arches. The equivalent footing at the east end was too badly robbed for any trace of superstructure to survive but here, too, one may assume a similar arrangement. The general effect of these internal divisions would have been to isolate the central part of the hall from the outside world, to give it a structure and feeling of unity and to prevent it from becoming a characterless tunnel leading through the wing.

One final refinement may be mentioned: in the western bay a small pool was built surrounded by a raised step and probably originally lined with sheets of marble. It was possible to trace the position of the water inlet, the size of the trench in which it was set suggesting a pipe of lead, leading to the centre of the pool where some form of fountain mechanism would have been adopted. The outfall, once composed of standard ceramic water pipes, was found leading to the ground level gutter surrounding the garden. A fountain in this position would have been visually very pleasing, particularly when viewed through the screen wall from the main hall. It would have focussed attention on the view beyond while at the same time emphasising the scale of the hall itself.

Apart from the structural consideration laid out above, we know very little of the interior decoration of the hall, largely because it was allowed to become ruinous during the Roman period and little now survives. Its floors, however, were of mortar while some at least of the walls were painted in panels of red. A marble cornice moulding was also recovered from the rubble but it need not necessarily have fallen from the adjacent superstructure. The general impression given by the surviving remains, however, is that the finish was not particularly exceptional. All the skill of the architect was centred upon the form of the superstructure, its contrived vistas, its volumes and its feelings of lightness. Carefully controlled proportions at the expense of decorative detail is a perfectly acceptable order of priorities in an entrance hall of this kind. A modern equivalent might be the entrance hall of a large railway station in which functional considerations are uppermost – no one would think of covering the walls of Waterloo Station with William Morris wallpaper. The analogy might be somewhat misleading, for there can be little doubt that the Fishbourne entrance hall was a brilliantly conceived structure, far superior to most of the Roman construction in this country.

The second large structural element in the East Wing was the aisled hall built at the north-east corner of the Palace in the angle between the East and North Wings, facing east. It was simpler in structure than the entrance hall, consisting of a single room 70 ft by 90 ft divided into a 'nave' and two side aisles by four pairs of massively constructed piers which would originally have supported two parallel arcades. All that now survives of the superstructure are two of the pier bases, single blocks of limestone 3 ft square and 12 ins thick. An examination of the foundations for the bases shows that they were all designed to support considerable weight, probably taking most of the vertical thrust from the roof, while the lateral thrust would have been absorbed by the side walls. Allowing for the tiles with which the roof was covered, the timber rafters and the rafter nails, a conservative estimate for the weight of the roof would be about 125 tons.

The structural details of the aisled hall would probably have been very much like those employed in the entrance hall with the central nave enclosed by a high ceiling, the aisles with somewhat lower ones but still high enough to allow large windows to be placed high up in the side walls, high because they would have had to be well above the adjacent roof lines, as the reconstruction drawing suggests, so as not to be obscured. The only entrance would have been in the centre of the east side, in front of which a massive pedimented front supported on six columns would almost certainly have been constructed to form an impressive façade to the building behind, and at the same time to balance with the façade of the entrance hall.

Fig. 27

Fig. 28
Plate 32

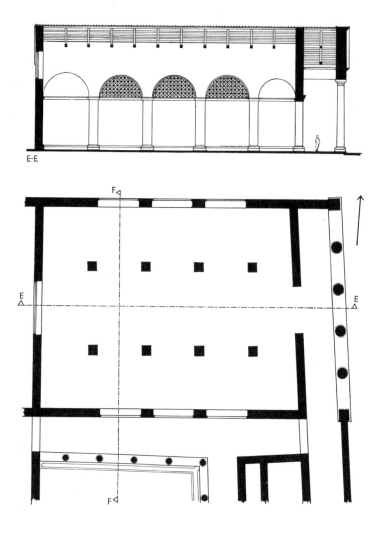

E-E

The function of the building is not altogether clear, but its comparative isolation from the rest of the Palace and the fact that it opens to the outside world suggests a semi-public use, and one strong possibility is that it served as an assembly hall similar to those found in Domitian's Palace. A place of assembly for the dependents of the estate and for the owner's low-ranking clients would have been essential in a Palace of this size. The siting of the aisled hall and its simple functional plan would have suited it admirably for this use.

An interesting series of alterations were made to the hall at an early stage in its life. Masonry pedestals were attached to the inner faces of the first three pairs of piers, and on the central axis of the far end a large masonry base was provided. These cannot have had anything to do with

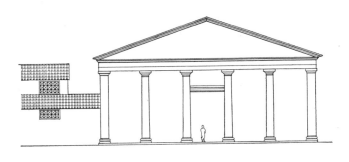

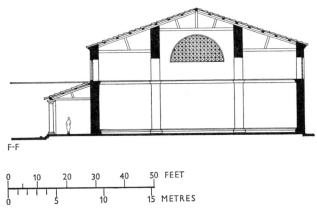

F-F

0 10 20 30 40 50 FEET
0   5   10   15 METRES

27, 28 Architectural reconstruction of the Aisled Hall in the north-east corner of the Palace

increasing the load-bearing capacity of the piers because their footings were too insubstantial, and indeed several of them showed some signs of subsidence. In fact, the general positioning leaves little doubt that they were in some way connected with visual embellishments, quite possibly supporting statues or, in the case of the central base, a group of statuary. This would have been quite in keeping with a place of public assembly. Indeed it is possible that the hall had religious overtones – a place where people might be expected to offer up public sacrifices for the wellbeing of the Emperor's household. The implications are extremely interesting but sadly beyond the scope of the archaeological evidence.

Between the aisled hall and entrance hall were two courtyards flanked by a range of eleven rooms. The northern courtyard, the larger of the two, was surrounded on three sides by a colonnaded veranda facing inwards towards a garden and closed on the fourth side by a blank wall. The southern courtyard was provided with colonnades along only two of its sides. Together the two gardens would have formed quiet open

Plates 33–35

spaces for walking and relaxation for the use of those residing in the range of rooms to the east.

The rooms themselves had all suffered very considerably from late Roman and post-Roman destruction and robbing, and apart from loose tesserae in room E6 and a few fragments of painted plaster in the style of that commonly found in the North Wing nothing of the interior decoration remains. The ground plan, however, is instructive. The rooms seem to have been deliberately built in suites consisting of one large and two smaller rooms, such as the groups made by E1–3, E4–6 and E9–11. Rooms E7 and 8 may possibly belong to a fourth set. Very similar arrangements are to be found in the official hotels (*mansiones*), particularly those at Richborough and Silchester.[24] It is probable that here, too, we are dealing with rooms for official travellers of low rank who could not expect to be offered the sumptuous guest suites in the North Wing. The East Wing suites were nevertheless comfortable and were, after all, provided with gardens even if they had to be shared with neighbours. Their only real disadvantage would have been the noise made by people using the entrance hall, the side street and the aisled hall.

The superstructure of this area is simple to reconstruct. The rooms would probably have been covered by a single pitched roof ending on gables before the walls of the two halls were reached.

The garden peristyles would have had the usual inward sloping type of roof supported on columns around the edge of the garden, and attached to the wall of the main range low enough to allow for windows into the rooms. Along the east side of the range ran a corridor leading between the porches of the entrance hall and aisled hall. It is difficult to be sure of its architectural treatment but there is some evidence to suggest that it was not colonnaded but was divided from the street by a plain blank wall provided with sufficient windows to allow in the necessary light. Such an arrangement would have given some privacy to the occupants of the range and cut down the volume of noise penetrating from outside.

South of the entrance hall the arrangement of the rooms and courtyards reflected as far as possible the plan on the north side. The peristyle of the proto-palace was retained largely intact to be an equivalent of the larger of the courtyards on the north, while a smaller courtyard seems to have been created between it and the hall to balance the smaller one on the other side of the hall. The range of rooms belonging to the old proto-palace was also retained and was continued up to the south side of the hall by a small block of new rooms.

How the baths themselves fared is difficult to say. There seem to have been comparatively few alterations except the extension of the room which contained the original *tepidarium*, but it must be admitted that several incompletely examined structures extend from the south side of the suite and that these may well belong to Flavian modifications.

The main structural elements of the Flavian Palace have now been summarized so far as the present evidence allows, but the building and its interior decoration is only one part of the complex. As we will see in the chapters to follow, they were set in a carefully constructed environment created with the same vision and skill as that lavished on the upstanding structures. Only when the surroundings have been described can we begin to appreciate the full significance of the whole conception.

VII

The Gardens and the Environment

Although in retrospect it is hardly surprising that a huge palatial building the size of that at Fishbourne should have been provided with gardens, it was not until 1964, three years after the start of the excavations, that the first traces of the formal garden began to appear, and it was not until the last season's work in April 1969 that the full extent of the southern garden became known. It was only when the question 'Was there a formal garden and if so is it discoverable by excavation?' was finally asked that the excavation became geared to providing the answers and the gardens were uncovered. That the Fishbourne gardens can be described in such detail is in part at least the result of asking questions, and not simply a feature of the uniqueness of the surviving remains. It would indeed be surprising if all other villas in this country were without traces of garden features.

In 1964 a trial trench was cut from the East Wing into the large central area enclosed by the four wings, specifically to examine the soil within the potential garden area. Much to our surprise, in addition to finding the original Roman top soil, three slots were discovered running parallel to the building and filled with a green loamy soil which had been marled with lime to counteract the slight acidity hereabouts. It looked very much as though these slots constituted some form of bedding trenches for plants, but before too much could be based on this it was necessary to see more of them in plan. In the following year, 1965, two areas were chosen for further examination of the garden problem, one in the northern part of the area and the other close to the north side of the entrance hall where, if the slots were bedding trenches, they might be expected to stop to allow access through the garden. The results were surprising, for not only were water pipes and posts of fences uncovered in the northern half, but the bedding trenches by the entrance hall were found to turn to form part of a façade apparently running across the garden and defining the north side of the path. The basic questions were therefore answered: there *was* a formal garden and it *was* discoverable by excavation. The next question to be asked 'What is the form of the garden?' took two years of consolidated effort to answer, but now for the first time in this country a Roman formal garden has been excavated.

Before considering the garden plan it is necessary to say something of the problems facing those who first laid it out and to describe the setting for their creation. We have already seen how at the time of the construction hundreds of tons of gravel and clay were shifted to create a level platform for the basic foundation of the North, East and South Wings and for the garden between them. This levelling must first have been preceded by the stripping of the topsoil and its stockpiling somewhere for re-use when the levelling was complete. Then clay and gravel was removed from the western part of the site and tipped over the lowlying eastern area to form the almost level platform. The result was the creation of an area 250 ft by 320 ft of barren, ill-drained clay hardly conducive to luxurious growth, but gradually, by a process of spreading the marled topsoil back over the clay and by digging deep bedding trenches whereever shrubs were to be planted, a hospitable environment was created in which, one hopes, the newly planted garden began to flourish.

The garden was completely surrounded by colonnaded walks, on the north, east and south, laid out at ground level and on the west side supported on the 5 ft high revetting wall. The colonnades were continuous and of a uniform height except at the centre of the west side, where steps led up to the porch of the audience chamber, and in the centre of the East Wing in front of the entrance hall, which was here provided with a monumental hexatyle façade. The general spacing of the columns of the colonnades is given by three which remain in position on the stylobate in the north-west corner of the garden, 11 ft apart. Elsewhere extensive robbing has removed not only the columns themselves but also the stylobate blocks and the ground level stone gutters in front. Knowing the spacing, however, and having sufficient pieces of their capitals and bases, it is possible to estimate that originally the columns were about 12 ft high, with the tiled roof of the veranda sloping up to the walls behind. The verandas were therefore high and wide.

The faces of the inner walls were plastered and painted. From the large quantity of fragments found in the north-west corner it is possible to show that, while still influenced by the concept of marble panelling, the decorators adopted a simplified and lighter style with a white dado splashed red and ochre surmounted by a plain white wall divided into panels with wide red bands, the panels being enlivened with simple diamond shaped inner frames painted in red or green. The entire scheme

Plate 40

Plates 36, 38

III   Aerial view of Fishbourne taken during the excavation of the garden. The modern building exactly covers the site of the Roman North Wing

IV   General view of the replanted garden as it is now, taken from the same position as Plate II, but four years later. Box bushes have been planted over the original Roman bedding trenches and a tree now stands in the position in which a bedding pit was discovered

V   Two bronze studs. One (top left) in the form of a human face, the other (top right) is decorated as a stylized lion's head. Below is an applied clay plaque representing a theatrical mask. It probably comes from the side of a pot. The objects are approximately full size

VI   Fragment of a Roman wall painting dating to the early Flavian period. It shows a colonaded villa against the background of the sea. An almost identical painting was found at Stabiae in Italy

VII   A detail of the Flavian mosaic pavement in room N 20

III

IV

V

VI

VII

must have been carefully chosen to suit the great expanse of wall presented by the verandas; it was sufficiently interesting to break the monotony but at the same time simple enough not to conflict with the sharp vertical emphasis of the colonnades. Like the painting elsewhere in the Palace it shows a fine regard for the overall visual context.

A certain structural problem was provided at the north-west (and presumably the south-west) corners of the garden where the low level colonnades of the North and South Wings abutted the higher level of the West Wing, but this was neatly overcome by providing a flight of timber steps between the two levels and raising the height of the lower colonnade in two steps by making the westernmost column about $2^1/_2$ ft higher, and of correspondingly larger diameter, and using it to support an architrave on different levels. In this way sufficient head-room was provided. With a certain embellishment of the roof-line at this point, perhaps with elaborate finials, the functional solution could have been turned to a positive visual advantage in enlivening the western façade and offering counterpoised points of interest balanced about the central audience chamber.

The presence of the veranda roofs sloping inwards towards the garden meant that great volumes of rainwater would have poured into the garden gutter which lay at ground level in front of the stylobate, a gutter composed of massive limestone and greensand slabs with a deeply hollowed upper surface. The garden was drained in two halves, the northern half towards the north-east corner and the southern half to one of the southern corners. The arrangement at the north-east corner shows that from here the water was led into a tile-built culvert, which passed beneath the veranda, and reappeared in the northern East Wing courtyard, running along the open gutter for a distance before disappearing again beneath the floor levels and the street in a culvert, which eventually opened into the canalized stream flanking the east side of the Palace complex. The course of the southern outfall may have been equally tortuous but the crucial area has not been excavated. The system is even more impressive when it is known that both of the North Wing courtyards as well as a small court on the north side of the entrance hall poured their contents out into the garden gutter through tile-built culverts laid beneath the verandas. Since the run-off from the adjacent roofs would also have found its way over the verandas and into the various courtyard gutters, it can be seen that at least half of the rain falling on the northern half of the Palace was drained from the building by the single culvert in

Fig. 29

Plate 42

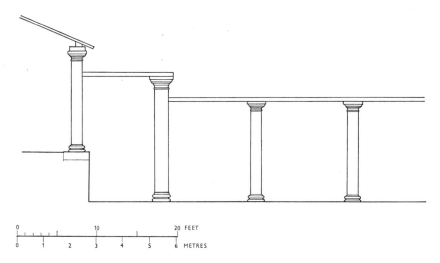

29 *The arrangement of the north colonnade in the north-west corner of the formal garden*

the north-east corner. The levelling of the drains was meticulously accurate – indeed it had to be: along the west front from the audience chamber steps to the north-west corner the fall was 0.77 ft (1 in 183) and from here to the north-east corner it was 1.80 ft (1 in 139). The capacity of the culvert also increased, that in the north-east corner having a cross section of 150 sq.ins. Even so it is difficult to believe that the system always functioned efficiently, particularly in the torrential downpours with which this part of the south coast is afflicted.

Fig. 30

So much then for the masonry backdrop to the garden, but what of the garden itself? The basic plan to which the gardeners worked was simple, a central path 40 ft wide was laid out across the garden from east to west, linking the entrance hall and audience chamber with the equivalent of a processional way, while subsidiary side paths were constructed to skirt the garden by running in front of the colonnades. All the paths were defined by bedding trenches.

Plates 37–39, 42

Plate II

The bedding trenches flanking the central path were arranged in a regular ornate fashion to create a series of large semicircular and rectangular recesses alternating with each other. Apart from the first and last recesses of the row, each was defined by two parallel bedding trenches, while the length of straight façade between them was composed of three trenches. If we are correct in assuming that the trenches supported con-Plate IVtinuous hedges of a shrub, like box, then either the multiple rows were allowed to grow together into one solid mass, or, more likely, they were kept clipped as individual hedges. In more recent gardens the same system is sometimes employed, the hedges often retaining banks of flowering plants. Such an arrangement could have been used at Fishbourne but it is impossible to discover relevant evidence; all that can be said is that a sufficient depth of soil was heaped up along the hedges to have allowed for interstitial planting. The centres of the recesses were carefully examined to see if trees or shrubs had been planted in them, but apart from the easternmost semicircular alcoves, where bedding pits indicate some form of growth, the others were without floral embellishment. Originally, however, they may well have been deliberately constructed to display groups of statuary, urns or other pieces of garden furniture, of which no archaeological trace need be expected to survive.

While the entire northern façade has been excavated, most of the southern side of the path lies beneath the gardens of modern houses where it is largely inaccessible. However, the first (easternmost) recess on the southern side lay within the excavation area and has proved to be almost an exact reflection of the northern side. Moreover, where, in one of the modern gardens, it was possible to check the western end of the façade again a close correspondence with the north side can be demonstrated. It seems reasonable therefore to assume on the present evidence, as the reconstruction plan does, that the centre path was symmetrically designed and laid out. An alternative arrangement might have allowed a subsidiary path to run from the centre of the main path to the centre of the South Wing if the construction of the wing demanded this kind of visual treatment, but since there is no shred of evidence in favour of the more elaborate view it is better at present to adopt the simpler hypothesis.

A great expanse of hedge-lined pathway running from one side of the garden to the other would have looked impressive enough, particularly with groups of statuary in the alcoves, but there were additional elaborations to give scale to the concept. On the central axis in front of the steps leading up to the audience chamber was found a square base made of tiles set in pink mortar, presumably part of a statue base. A single figure standing here on a raised plinth would have looked magnificent against the columns of the audience chamber. In an equivalent position at the east end of the path a substantial soil-filled pit was found, but there is no evidence of its date or function. Its regular spacing in relation to the main east-west axis would imply that it was constructed as part of the garden layout but what manner of superstructure it took is beyond recovery.

From the west end of the central path, side paths ran along the front of the West Wing; the one on the north has been completely excavated. It was about 12 ft wide and lined on both sides with hedges represented now by bedding trenches of the same kind as those delineating the central path. On the east side, against the central area of the garden, two trenches had been dug, the one nearest the path kinking in at regular intervals towards a straight one behind. The trenches on the west side, towards the building, were more complex in layout, consisting of two parallel straight lines with a third, close to the edge of the path, returning at regular intervals to meet the middle trench, creating small recesses equivalent to those on the opposite side. One particularly interesting feature of these western trenches is that the rows were of differing depths, the deepest being against the wall, possibly implying that the hedges were intended to be of increasing height. It is tempting here to remember the description which Pliny gives of his Tuscan garden,[25] in which he says that one of the garden walls was hidden behind banks of hedges which gradually increased in height towards the wall.

It was evident at Fishbourne that the revetting wall for the West Wing was regarded as a structural feature to be hidden. This was done by plastering the wall, painting it a uniform deep green background colour, and over this painting a range of vegetation including great leafy fronds and stems with tendrils growing up them. Behind these an on-looker was allowed to glimpse a garden scene beyond with its garden features of lattice-work picked out in white. In fact the West Wing wall was camouflaged to give the impression of yet another garden.

The western bedding trenches, in front of the revetting wall, ended with a large pit which had been deliberately dug into the clay and filled with garden soil. A close examination of the sides of the pit suggested the possibility that roots had penetrated out into the clay implying the presence of a substantial growth, probably a tree. Visually a tree here would have been highly acceptable, partly to obscure the slight incongruity in the different levels of the colonnade roof and partly to hide the water tank (which will be described later, p. 139). It would also have added an attractive emphasis to the end of the West Wing colonnade and would presumably have been balanced by another at the south-west corner.

The path along the north side of the garden was very much like the west path except that the recesses in the garden-side hedge were omitted. The east path was, however, altogether different, for while a façade of bedding trenches was maintained in front of the colonnade there were no bedding trenches along the garden side of the path except for shallow discontinuous slots which could have resulted from the planting of small herbaceous flowers. In fact the central area of the garden was open to the east path, unlike the other three sides where hedges intervened.

While the north half of the garden has been almost totally excavated, very little work has been possible in the southern half except over the eastern side where a strip of land was available for excavation. Here limited trial trenching has shown that the bedding trenches along the east colonnade reflect those on the north side, but features equivalent to the north path do not appear to be in place along the south. Rather more excavation will be needed before the problem of this south side can be cleared up.

The garden, then, was divided by means of hedge-lined paths into two halves which could have been laid out either with a vast wilderness of vegetation like that shown on the famous wall painting in the Garden Room of Livia at the Prima Porta, or it could have been kept as short-mown grass. On balance the evidence would seem to point to grass, partly because luxuriant vegetation would have obscured the carefully contrived views and partly because in spite of extensive and careful excavation of most of the central area only one solitary bedding pit was discovered: it is most unlikely therefore that deep rooted plants could have grown in the area.

The one bedding pit is very carefully sited so that the tree which it supported would have appeared towards the centre of the line of vision of a person standing in the centre of the West Wing and looking towards the North Wing. Anyone who stands here today can appreciate the value of the tree which has been replanted on this spot, in relieving the monotony of the front of the North Wing – the strong vertical emphasis of a mature tree is exactly what is needed to counteract the horizontality of the wing. This point raises an even more important one: how was the front of the East Wing enlivened when viewed from the west? Structurally the centre was provided with the pedimented front of the entrance hall but on each side was a continuous and highly repetitive colonnade stretching for 130 ft; such visual boredom would have been intolerable, but in the hands of the brilliant landscape gardener the problem was overcome with simple elegance. The bedding trench closest to the east colonnade was filled not with the marled loam used elsewhere, but with a thick black occupation rubbish of the kind which the elder Pliny suggests was suitable for bedding roses. This fact, taken in conjunction with a number of post-holes hereabouts which imply some form of timber structure, possibly lattice-work, strongly suggests that a type of climbing

Plate 41

Plate IV

plant was grown here to some height. A further point, apparent on the plan, is that the outer bedding trench, which for part of its length turned back on the middle trench in the manner of the trenches elsewhere, was replaced by a straight trench along the south part of the path and was associated with post-holes. Here again the implication is of a different type of vegetation, possibly climbers arranged so that the façade became denser as the central path was approached. If this were done on the south side as well, the contrast, where the thick façades of vegetation suddenly gave place to a clear view of the front of the entrance hall beyond, would have been very exciting.

Yet this was not all: 35 ft in front of the colonnade a second screen was created of trees alternating with substantial upright timbers, represented now by bedding pits of black soil and stone-packed post-holes. There can be very little doubt that we are dealing here with evidence of some kind of flowering tree which it was necessary to train along a timber frame-work. The younger Pliny writing of one of his gardens describes how in one place there was 'a row of fruit trees alternating with posts to give an air of rural simplicity in surroundings of otherwise studied formality.[26] Rural simplicity is hardly a term which could be used of the Fishbourne garden but nevertheless this kind of arrangement was clearly widely prac-tised in the Roman world. Again it will be seen that the function of this screen was to add interest to the view looking east and by returning the posts for a short distance along the north side the eastern façade was cleverly integrated with the rest of the building. This is yet another ex-ample of the landscape gardener's great skill.

Nothing has yet been said of the plants growing in the garden. It was at one stage hoped that pollen analysis of the soil from the bedding trenches would throw some light on the problem, but the conditions were not conducive to pollen survival and all that remained were a few grains of the tougher pollen such as hawkweed, daisy and other weeds of cul-tivation. We have therefore to rely on classical sources, both literature and painting, to give some idea of what might have been grown. In Italy the favourite hedging plant, referred to constantly by Pliny, was box which is known to have grown in Britain during the Roman period. The care-ful marling of the soil in the bedding trenches for the Fishbourne hedges would have created ideal conditions for the shrub, but while the presence of box is *likely* we cannot be certain of its use here. Other plants would probably have included roses and fruit trees, as we have seen, and there may have been a host of other smaller flowers including perhaps rosemary, lilly and acanthus – all popular flowers in the Roman period. When the deep waterlogged silts in the harbour have been fully analysed it might well be possible to trace the more delicate pollen grains of the garden flowers which, in theory at least, could have survived under these conditions. Then, and only then, it may be possible to think of the garden in terms of its colours and its scent.

One of the more surprising discoveries was that the garden was supplied with fresh water by means of an extensive, and no doubt expensive, system of ceramic pipes set beneath the paths. The water appears to have been derived from a spring in the north-east corner of the site and taken, presumably from a raised tank sited somewhere there, by means of an aquaduct along the north wall of the North Wing, then along the west wall, into a settling tank built in the north-west corner of the garden. Part of the aquaduct, constructed of roof tiles in clay and mortar, still survives but unfortunately by some strange coincidence it lay almost exactly in the path of the 1960 watermain trench and was largely destroyed by it. The last length of the supply, passing through the corner of the West Wing to the tank, was conducted by means of ceramic water pipes set in a clay-lined trench to prevent leakage. The tank was built on a stone foundation which projected into the corner of the garden. Originally it would have been of timber, perhaps lined with lead, but no trace of the superstructure has survived. The function of a tank in this position was two-fold: to form a reservoir with a sufficient head of water to serve the garden and to allow sediment to settle out. This last point was of particular importance because had muddy water been allowed into the pipes they would soon have become blocked, causing serious problems.

From the tank the water was fed into several ceramic pipe-lines embedded in the clay beneath the path. Each pipe-line was composed of individual pipes 18 ins long and 8 ins in diameter with an internal bore of 4 ins. Their ends were so made that one socketed neatly into the other, making a firm joint which was then sealed with a hard white mortar. The first pipe-line ran along the north edge of the north path and turned at right-angles in the north-east corner to take up a similar position along the east side as far as the central path, where the main pipe stopped and a subsidiary branch led to the pool in the entrance hall. The function of the pipe was clear enough: it was designed to take water to a series of basins or fountains placed along the path, possibly in the recesses in the hedges. The second pipe ran along the centre of the north and east paths, apparently completely untapped (because most of the eastern length of

Plate 39

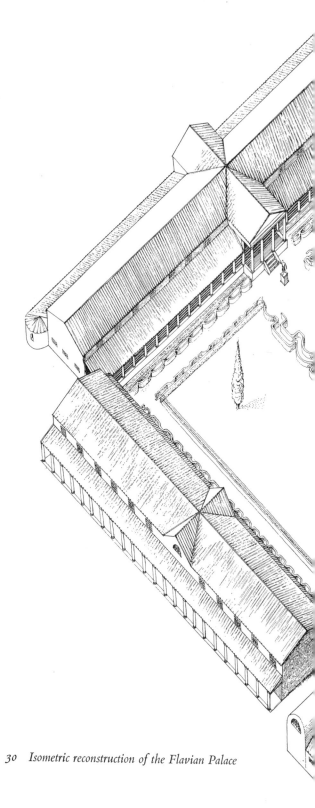

30   Isometric reconstruction of the Flavian Palace

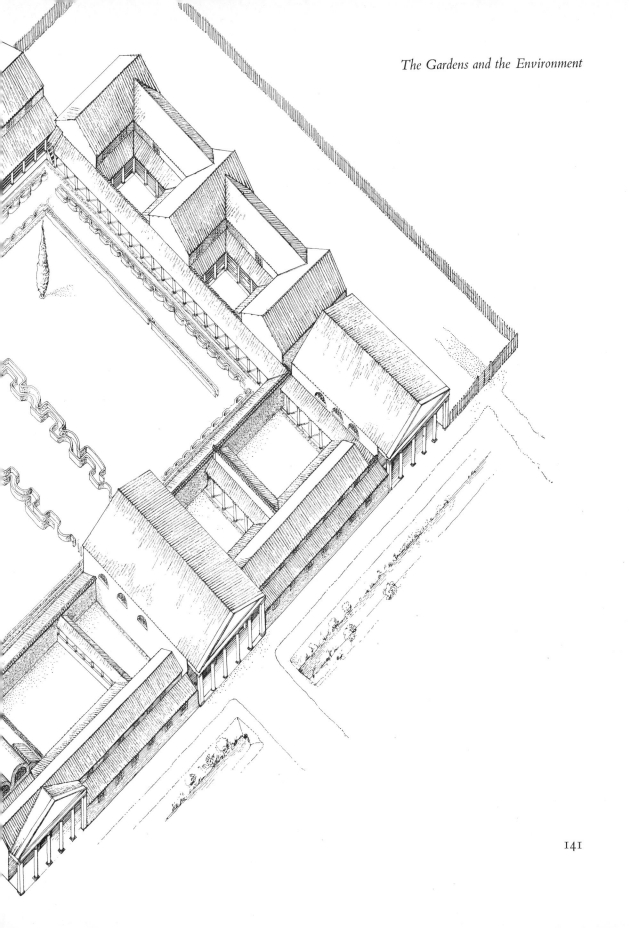

pipe was still intact), but after crossing the central path it veered towards the hedge and from here on it presumably served the fountains lining the path. It had, in fact, taken over the function of the first pipe in the southern part of the garden. The point is an interesting one because it shows that while the tank could provide a sufficient head of water to service a considerable number of fountains, its energy had been spent by the time the entrance hall was reached. The southern part of the garden had therefore to be provided with a separate supply, running untapped until it reached the south of the central path. A third pipe ran from the tank south along the west path, apparently serving fountains along the entire length of the West Wing. How the south side of the garden was supplied, whether by the continuation of the second or third pipe or a combination of both, is not known.

We have referred to fountains and basins arranged along the paths but it must be admitted that no structure of this kind has been found in position. This is not, however, surprising for the building had a long life after the great garden had ceased to be used, during which time the pilfering of objects such as basins and their lead fittings probably took place. Since they would have needed no footing, little trace can be expected to remain. Fragments of several of the basins have, however, survived in rubble deposits about the Palace. The most substantial of these is a semi-circular basin more than 3 ft in diameter carved from a solid slab of Purbeck marble. A basin of this kind would probably have been set at ground-level with water gently bubbling into it. A fragment of a more elaborate basin was found discarded in a late well cut through one of the East Wing courtyards; again it was carved from Purbeck marble but it seems to have once been provided with legs slotted into the underside. No doubt a wide variety of different types were in use, as indeed contemporary wall paintings of Roman gardens suggest. When the fountains at Fishbourne were turned on there would have been no spouts of water gushing high in the air, but instead gentle streams bubbling up in the basins laid around the paths, the waste water flowing away into the gutters behind the hedges.

Enough has been said of the great formal garden to give some idea of its Roman form and the way in which it was meticulously contrived to fit into, and indeed enhance, the surrounding Palace. It was essentially a show-piece, there to set off the building to the amazement of visitors. It was nothing less than a piece of window dressing to demonstrate to a second generation Roman Province the sophistication of true Roman culture.

The formal garden enclosed within the wings of the Palace was essentially a semi-public area open to all visitors, but as we have seen it was only the West Wing, itself the official range, which opened onto it. The rooms of the North Wing and of the residential parts of the East Wing were provided with their own private gardens surrounded with quiet colonnaded walks. One has only to read Pliny's description of his gardens in Italy to understand how a sensitive Roman appreciated them; wandering around he was delighted by their surprising contrasts, by the soft grass beneath his feet, by the interplay of light and shade in a wooded glade; it was nature itself that Pliny loved, not human contrivance.[27] It is no surprise then that when we turn away from the formal garden to examine the huge private garden stretching southwards from the South Wing of the Palace we find not the rigid structure of the garden to the north but a great naturalness.

In the previous chapter we saw how the details of the South Wing were reconstructed from fragments and how they demonstrated that the wing, possibly the residential wing belonging to the owner, faced south across a colonnaded veranda to the sea. The excavation of 1967 showed that an artificial terrace existed, but it was not until 1969 that it became possible to examine the area in any detail. The land was divided between a modern building estate, a derelict chicken farm and a strip of pasture belonging to the Church Commissioners. At Easter 1969 trial trenches were dug within the chicken farm to test its potential while a careful watch was kept on the construction trenches opened on the building site. Under these rather unpromising conditions details of the Roman layout gradually came to light, but much more work remains to be done and will be done in the next few years.

We now know that an artificial terrace was constructed for a distance of about 300 ft south of the wing ending, at its south edge, on a quay wall of stone blocks and timber, beyond which lay the sea. How the sea water was retained in the huge lagoon-like inlet has not yet been defined, but some kind of mole built out across the harbour end probably kept the water back at low tide while the constant flow from the fresh water streams maintained the level. Lock gates must have been provided in the mole to allow ships to sail up to the terrace. This much is suggested by the construction of a channel 30 ft wide dredged along the terrace edge – clearly the intention was to provide a 5–6 ft depth of water so that quite large vessels could come close in.

The terrace itself seems to have been laid out as a 'natural' garden. At one point a shallow stream was found flowing into a large pond constructed towards the centre of the area. An artificial water supply was also piped into the western side of the garden, where there were no convenient natural springs to tap. Elsewhere the made-up surface is penetrated with short lengths of bedding trenches and isolated bedding pits, apparently laid out haphazardly, suggesting the shrubs and trees had been planted at random to produce the impression of gently sloping parkland leading down to the sea. The inlet at this point would have been about 400 ft wide and on the opposite side the land sloped up again. Here careful tree planting could have created a superb enclosing landscape with wooded areas giving way gradually to a seashore. Even now, with all the modern development to which the area has been subjected, it is possible to recapture something of its former peaceful atmosphere.

Fig. 31

There is still a lot to be learnt about this southern 'natural' garden: was it, for example, closed on the east and west sides by colonnades or at least some kind of wall or fence? This might be expected but it has not yet been proved. The deep water silts which clogged the lagoon after the garden was abandoned are of particular interest because under these waterlogged conditions organic material is preserved. Already leather shoes, a wooden bowl and a wooden comb have been recovered, together with large quantities of pottery, some of it with food residues inside. When this part of the site has been fully excavated and the finds studied, we will have learnt much of those aspects of environment and life which, under normal archaeological conditions, are very seldom recoverable.

Plate 83

The Palace, as we have so far described it, covered about 10 acres but it lay within a much larger complex which must have included estate buildings such as workshops, kitchens, store rooms and servants' quarters. Some idea of the layout is at last beginning to emerge. The Palace was approached by a wide road leading due west from Chichester to the east front of the entrance hall, where it joined a service road, or street, which flanked the entire east façade of the building, running from the inlet north to beyond the front of the aisled hall. At this point the road turned at right-angles and ran through the centre of a fenced enclosure, north of the North Wing, to the general working yards west of the Palace.

This northern enclosure, some 80 ft wide, had been carefully levelled up with tips of gravel and clay at the time when the Palace was laid out. Its northern limit was marked by a series of large fence posts which prob-

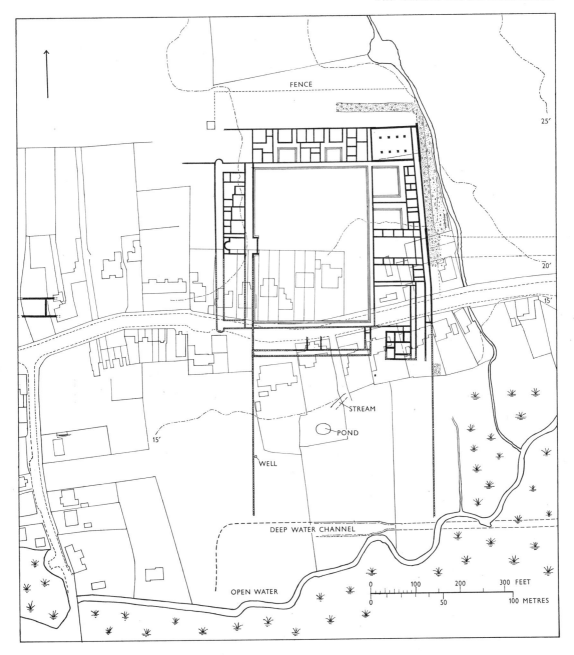

FENCE

25′

20′

15′

15′

STREAM

POND

WELL

DEEP WATER CHANNEL

OPEN WATER

| 0 | | 100 | | 200 | | 300 FEET |

| 0 | | 50 | | 100 METRES |

31   *The extent of the Flavian Palace, as it is at present known, in relation to the modern village*

ably served as the basis of a close boarded fence dividing the immediate territory of the Palace from the land beyond. Levelling over the eastern part of the enclosure had raised the surface by 4–5 ft above the valley floor. To the north, where there was no make-up, a substantial marshy area formed, drained only by the canalized stream which ran along the eastern limit of the Palace. With the marsh on the north, stream to the east and sea to the south, the Palace would have looked impressively isolated.

Most of this northern enclosed area has not been extensively excavated but parts of several buildings are known to lie within. The western part of the enclosure, however, was totally examined before the present museum, concourse and service buildings were erected, and several interesting features have come to light. The angle between the North and West Wings was covered with a thickness of black soil containing churned-up occupation rubbish, suggesting the possibility of a well-manured garden. Kitchen gardens were a favourite adjunct to all private villas and houses in Italy and indeed have a much longer ancestry than the formal and decorative gardens which became popular only during the period of Hellenization in the first century BC. The kitchen garden was traditional to Rome, it was here that the herbs were grown to flavour the food and flowers and plants were cultivated for offering to the gods on the household and public shrines. It is quite probable that this north-west corner of cultivated land at Fishbourne was the kitchen garden. We know that it was provided with a supply of fresh water led to the centre of the area by a wooden water pipe joined to the aquaduct. Such a provision would have been essential to water the plants during the summer, when this part of the site would have dried out.

Close to the edge of the garden area was the base of a large masonry bread oven of the kind found in the bakery at Pompeii. It was a complex affair with air vents and raking channels at the bottom, which still survive, and the main flue and oven chamber at a convenient working height above. An installation of this size would have been able to serve the needs of the entire Palace. Its siting, here in the open, is not at all surprising – Roman bakeries of this size were open air structures. When all the factors are considered, the Fishbourne bakery can be seen to have been very carefully situated. It needed to be close to the building it served, within easy reach of the road supplying it, near a water supply and not too far from the servants' quarters. It satisfied all these conditions admirably. We may assume that cart-loads of corn were brought into the enclosure along the service road and off-loaded into storage buildings. The grain was then ground into flour somewhere in this area. The exact site of the mill has not yet been identified but a massive grindstone of German lava was discovered here by workmen laying a drain. It was too large to have been rotated by hand and must therefore have come from a large establishment employing some form of simple machinery. Once the flour had been produced and stored, it could be drawn upon as and when necessary for the production of the bread.

The entire production sequence of the baking process was thus centralized in this northern enclosure, but we do not yet know where the rest of the cooking was carried out. Fairly elaborate kitchens would have been needed to provide food for the sumptuous banquets which must have been held in the Palace and since no suitable accommodation has been found within the Palace as it is now known, we must suppose that the kitchens as well as the servants' quarters lay somewhere to the west. Unfortunately this area is now beneath the densest part of the modern village and large-scale excavation is impossible. Limited trial trenching some 300 ft west of the West Wing has, however, brought to light part of a substantial range of rooms built in the same style of masonry as the main Palace. Here, presumably, are the domestic ranges tucked away out of sight behind the Palace so as not to detract from its grandeur.

The discovery is interesting because it raises the whole problem of the housing of the vast army of servants who would have been needed to maintain a building of this size. Estimates of numbers are impossible because we do not know whether the Palace estates as well as the building itself were administered from here, but in all probability they were, in which case the installations must have covered many acres. In addition to kitchens and servants' accommodation, there would probably have been provision for all kinds of estate production and maintenance, storage facilities for raw materials and export commodities, in fact the entire administrative network required to run what must have been a vast enterprise.

Although positive evidence of this fascinating aspect of the Palace complex is at present lacking, it can be said that the area immediately west of the Palace was admirably suited to such a function. A large tract of good dry land was available between the Palace and the marshy valley now marked by Salthill Lane, stretching down to the western inlet of the harbour. Casual observations made over the years have shown that some reclaimation of the harbour fringes did take place during the Roman period and a mass of Roman debris has been recovered from the Mill Pond which marks the exact position of the western channel. Already plans are in hand for the gradual exploration of the area and it may not be too long before the details of the estate yard and its harbour begin to emerge.

44, 45 One of the earliest changes to be made to the Flavian palace was the laying of a new mosaic floor in room 13 of the North Wing. The design was lively, incorporating a Medusa's head as a centre-piece, but the style of workmanship was somewhat uneven and several mistakes were made in the layout (see *Fig. 33*). Some parts of the floor had been ploughed away, *right*, leaving only the mortar matrix. When this was removed part of an earlier, Flavian, mosaic in black and white was seen below

46, 47   Sea-horses from the 'dolphin mosaic'

48–50 Details from the 'dolphin mosaic'. *Above*, the cupid and dolphin centrepiece (see Plate I); *below, left*, one of the vases used as infilling; *below, right*, a small bird shown on one of the tendrils of the border

51, 52   Sea-panthers from the 'dolphin mosaic'

53 General view across the floors of the North Wing, looking east from room N9

54 Third-century mosaic in room N8 of the North Wing

55, 56 Two of the second-century mosaics from the North Wing of the palace. The floor, *above*, may depict a peacock, of which only the feet and splayed tail survive. *Left*, is a simple geometric panel from the centre of a room

57 The floor in room N 14 was > relaid during the second century in a style closely similar to the Flavian mosaic in room N 12 nearby. This concious copying implies that the pattern was still acceptable to the later occupants

58–60 A general view of the west end of the North Wing, *above*, showing the arrangement to-wards the end of the third century, by which time the palace had reached its final form. The latest alteration to be made was the addition of a heating system to the corner room (*opposite, above*). In the centre of the room was the pillared hypocaust served by a flue (*opposite, below*) from a stoking chamber. Diagonal flues led to the corners of the room to chimneys set in the walls. Excavation showed that the heating arrangements were never used and were apparently unfinished

61 The west courtyard in the North Wing before conservation

62 The basement of a pillared hypocaust inserted into room N 8 in the third century

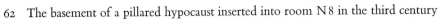

63 The second-century bath suite, built into the East Wing of the palace, possessed a substantial cold swimming bath, shown here. The masonry of the walls has been robbed away but the floor, of re-used tile and slabs of marble, is well preserved. In one corner and along one wall was a bench to allow the bather to sit with feet dangling in the water

64, 65 The Roman well, in the southern courtyard of the East Wing, at two different stages of excavation. *Above*, is the well as it appeared when the filling of the shaft had been taken out. The lower photograph shows a later stage after the packing of the well pit had been removed. The timber lining can be clearly seen

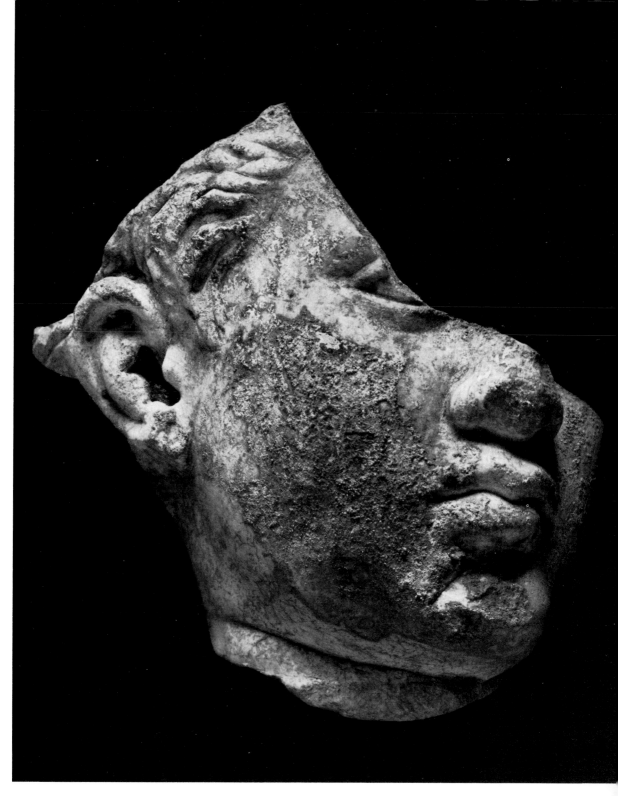

66 A marble head of a youth found in a late rubble deposit in the North Wing. The piece is of continental workmanship of late first-century date. The subject is a young man, originally wearing a metal helmet, with somewhat sullen features. It is a portrait study, in all probability of one of the owner's children

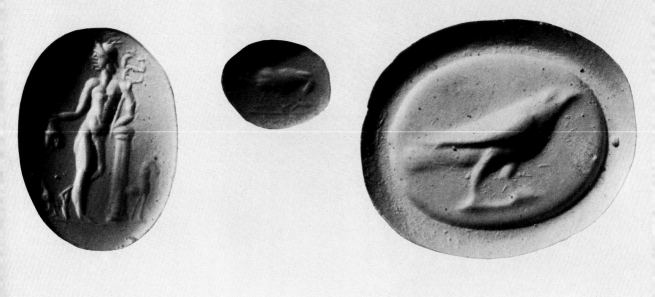

67 Three of the gemstones found in the palace: *left*, an amethyst depicting Hermes, engraved in exceptionally fine style: *centre*, a green stone from a child's ring, simply engraved with a bird; *right*, a green glass intaglio bearing a representation of a raven, a symbol of good luck

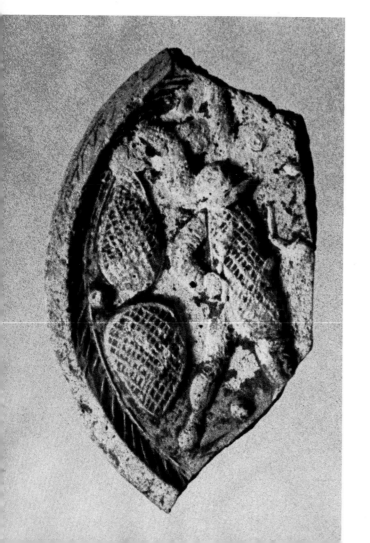

68 An applied plaque from the side of a pottery flask of a type manufactured in Western France in the first century AD. This particular fragment shows a scene from a gladiatoral combat. Plaques of this kind are rare in Britain

69 A fragment of painted wall plaster scratched with the letters ...] S DAB.M [... ...] XVM, meaning, 'I was giving'. A sign of literacy in the first century

70 Part of a frieze of moulded stucco from the North Wing of the palace. The design is repetitive, showing two birds with fruit in their beaks standing on either side of vases of fruit (see *Fig. 23*). The moulding probably came from the junction of wall and ceiling

71 A fragment of an unusual pottery vessel which was probably decorated with a human face, wearing a crown in the form of a city wall. The surviving fragment from Fishbourne shows the wall, a gate and a scar to which a moulded bastion had once been attached. The vessel may have had some religious significance

72 The thighs and drapery of a small pipe-clay figurine of Venus. Votive figurines of this kind were mass-produced in Britain and are frequently found on Roman sites

VIII

The Owner and his Changing Fortunes

A modern architect asked to give an estimate for building the Palace using the cheapest modern methods, without any allowance for the interior decorations, suggested that it would cost about three-quarters of a million pounds. Add to this an equivalent sum for the gardens, the painting, the marble work and the mosaics, and we have an order of magnitude of about one and half million pounds. A house costing this much today would be exceptional – so it was in the Roman period.

In the contemporary Romano-British countryside there would have been nothing like it. The average upper class farmhouse, like those found at Lockleys and Park Street, were little bungalows of 5 or 6 rooms totalling no more than 60 ft in length. Both of them together would have fitted into the courtyard in the East Wing. There were a few, more substantial, houses like the villa now being excavated at Eccles in Kent and like Angmering and the Fishbourne proto-palace, but these in no way compare to the size of the Flavian Palace. By the middle of the fourth century larger establishments had grown up but even one of the largest, the villa at Woodchester in the Cotswolds, could have been fitted, courtyards and all, into the formal garden. Moreover these big fourth-century villas were usually the result of a gradual growth, sometimes beginning a century or two earlier, and included storage space and servants' quarters as well. The Fishbourne Palace was planned and erected at one time.

Monumental masonry buildings were not, however, unknown in Britain in the late first century. In the Flavian period the country was in the throes of a massive programme of urban expansion. Everywhere monumental public buildings were being erected. The great forum and basilica arrangements in Cirencester and Verulamium were known to be of this date, the first phase of the bathing establishment at Bath was by now underway, and recently a huge palatial building, possibly the governor's or procurator's residence, has come to light in London. This was, of course, all part of a deliberate policy, followed by the Flavian governors of Britain, to Romanize the province with a vengeance. Tacitus described it clearly enough.[28] When writing of the work of the governor Agricola, he says: 'To induce a people hitherto scattered, uncivilized and therefore prone to fight, to grow pleasurably inured to peace and ease Agricola gave private encouragement and official assistance to the building of temples, fora and private villas ... And so the Britons were gradually led on to the amenities that make vice agreeable – arcades, baths and sumptuous banquets. They spoke of such novelties as civilization when really they were only a feature of their enslavement.' It was in the midst of this atmosphere that the Palace was built. It is clear enough from what Tacitus has to say, and from the evidence of the archaeological record, that much of the country was in the grip of a monumental building craze, which would of course have offered an incentive to skilled foreign craftsmen to come to Britain. But while this may have provided the means whereby the Fishbourne Palace was built, it does not explain the motivation. One could offer 'private encouragement and official assistance' to private individuals to build their houses in the Roman manner, but it would need a very powerful and wealthy man to translate such encouragement into a building like Fishbourne. What, then, must concern us is not the general climate of opinion that allowed it but the man who demanded it. Who was he and why build such a place? It must be admitted that there is no incontrovertible evidence nor, short of an inscription, is there ever likely to be. All we can do is to weigh the possibilities. There are three: that it was built for, or by, a high ranking Roman official; that it belonged to a Roman speculator investing money in the province; or that it belonged to a rich local landowner. The simplest solution would be to suppose that it was the work of Cogidubnus who fits each and all of the possibilities, he was a *legatus augusti*, a wealthy Roman citizen and a local client king. But even more important, Fishbourne lay close to the centre of the territory over which he ruled; for anyone else to have lived in such style only a mile from his capital would have been a great insult to a loyal friend of Rome.

The further the evidence is examined, the more it points to Cogidubnus. First of all there is the development of building at Fishbourne. The first residential structure which has been recognized is the large timber house with its workshops, probably built within a decade of the invasion. In size and decoration it was well above contemporary standards and clearly belonged to a person of some wealth. Later, during the reign of Nero, it was replaced by a far more sumptuous building constructed now in masonry, and while it did not increase the size of the establishment to any great extent it incorporated a number of new expensive Roman luxuries such as a peristyle and a bath suite. The relationship of the two buildings suggests that one replaced the other in a manner which points to a continuity of ownership. Exactly the same can be said of the Flavian building which strictly can be thought of as a gross extension of the earlier proto-palace, still retained largely intact in the corner of the new complex. It looks, then, as though one thread of ownership runs through the entire development from the 40's and 50's to the 70's and 80's, but as we will see in the next chapter the thread seems to have been broken before the end of the first century, when some reversal of fortune can be detected.

The plan of the Palace discussed in the previous chapters gives some hint of the type of function for which it was built. Three elements may be isolated: a private residential aspect (the South Wing), an official and semi-public section (the West Wing, entrance hall and aisled hall) and the residential apartments for visitors (the North Wing and parts of the East). It must therefore have been a building occupied by an official of considerable status who needed to provide adequate accommodation for visiting dignitaries. But it is the audience chamber that really emphasises his status. A man allowed to build such a room for himself, a room clearly reflecting the audience chambers of the Emperors, must have been not only rich and important but also thoroughly backed by the Roman government.

How then does what little we can deduce of the career of Cogidubnus fit within this framework? We have already shown that he was probably a member of the native ruling household, at the time of the invasion in AD 43, who was chosen to remain leader of the tribe with the status of a client king after the invasion as a reward for his and his tribe's support at the conquest.[29] At about this time he was made a Roman citizen, taking the names of the Emperor Tiberius Claudius as a mark of his respect. So far there is nothing remarkable: dozens of young men all over the Roman world were in similar positions. Yet at some stage, presumably later, he was given the surprising title of *legatus augusti*, recorded on the Chichester inscription.[30] For a native king to be given such a high rank in the Roman aristocracy was almost unheard of, apart from the case of King Herod whose status at one stage was broadly similar. It has been suggested[31] that Cogidubnus' elevation took place in 48 when Claudius is accused of opening the ranks of the senate to Gauls. Claudius was certainly at pains to integrate worthy provincials into the governmental hierarchy, but there must have been many more highly qualified for such an honour

Plate 32

than the young and virtually untried Cogidubnus. This, then, was hardly the occasion. Another context for loyalty and reward would have been during the rebellion of Boudicca in AD 60 when much of eastern Britain was in revolt against Rome. A stable south-east firmly under the control of the pro-Roman king would have been welcome to the military authorities, but no incident involving Cogidubnus is singled out for special mention and it may be that his territory was not involved.

A far more serious situation would have arisen in AD 69, the Year of the Four Emperors when, following the death of Nero, the Empire was thrown into turmoil whilst the contenders for the throne fought it out with each other. At the end of the struggle Vespasian emerged triumphant, but not without the support of many loyal friends. In Britain the legions were not heavily involved in the struggle but they tended to support Vitellius. It is, however, by no means impossible that Cogidubnus, who would surely have known Vespasian as a young commander in AD 43, lent his support to the future Emperor perhaps significantly swaying the opinion of the civil population. This is pure speculation but is well within the realms of possibility.

Once firmly in power Vespasian is known to have handed out unprecedented rewards to his supporters. One man, L. Autistius Rusticus, *tribunus laticlavius* of the second legion (Vespasian's old legion still stationed in Britain) was appointed a legionary legate at this time, this rapid elevation giving him the right to sit in the Senate. There would have been nothing unusual in upgrading Cogidubnus, a faithful ally of Rome for more than a quarter of a century, to the position of *legatus augusti* at the same time. When Tacitus, writing in about AD 98 says that he 'maintained his unswerving loyalty down to our own time', he may well have been referring to a specific act of faith in 69 when he himself was a boy of 12 or 13. In summary, we can say that of the three occasions when Cogidubnus might have distinguished himself in the eyes of Rome sufficiently to be rewarded with the title of *legatus augusti*, in 43, 60 and 69, 69 has the strongest claim. At any event, by the time that the temple to Neptune and Minerva was being erected, in the early Flavian period at the latest, if the style of lettering is anything to go by, Cogidubnus had reached the peak of his career.

How then does this interpretation of the man's fortunes fit the development of the Fishbourne Palace? The timber house and the proto-palace spanning the 50's and 60's would have provided perfectly adequate accommodation for a client king, the elaboration of the proto-palace reflecting an increase in spending power and a desire to go Roman, without noticably altering the size of the basic establishment. The major change came in the mid-70's with the enormous extension of the residence to its palatial form. It is tempting to link this event with the elevation of Cogidubnus to the senatorial rank of *legatus augusti*. The new building was a palace fit for a senator.

We do not know when the old king died, but guessing that he may have been in his early twenties at the time of the invasion he would have reached his 70's by the last decade of the century, which it is unlikely that he outlived. With the death of a client king Roman policy was clear; his kingdom reverted to the state; client kingdoms were not perpetuated. Therefore before the first century was out the *regnum* of Cogidubnus had probably become part of the Empire. It is surely no coincidence that it is at this time that marked changes can be detected in the status of the building, the money or the desire to maintain it at its former level were no longer available.

We are most unlikely ever to know for certain who owned Fishbourne. A strong case can be made out for Cogidubnus but it is essentially a case based on possibilities: this is one of the fascinations of the subject. All that can fairly be said is that it is easier to argue that Cogidubnus was the owner than that he was not.

In the half century or so following the turmoil of the invasion period the kingdom had been converted into a worthy part of the Roman Empire. Its cantonal capital at Chichester by now possessed a street grid, a forum and basilica, an amphitheatre, a temple to the honour of the Divine House and probably a large public bathing establishment. It was adorned with statues to the emperor and the gods – all known from the archaeological evidence. The surrounding countryside, particularly the coastal plain, was equally advanced with its numerous masonry villas belonging to the wealthy native landowners, men whose fathers had probably taken sides in the conflicts of Verica's time. And here at Fishbourne a mile from the town lay a palace which must have taken the breath away from even the most sophisticated Roman visitor. All this was a fair return for the backing the Romans had given to a virtually unknown Briton way back in the 40's.

IX

The Second Century

Throughout the second and third centuries changes, sometimes minor sometimes sweeping, can be detected in the structure of the old palace. Gradually as time went on less and less attention was paid to the West, East and South Wings and all the effort went into improving the inhabited area, which by the third century centred upon the west end of the North Wing.

Fig. 32

The first major change came at the beginning of the second century, when the aisled hall was modified and a bath suite was inserted into the passageway between the hall and the east end of the North Wing. Why such an addition should have been required is difficult to say, because the south-east baths were probably still in good working order. One possibility is, of course, that the Palace was now divided between two owners, each requiring their own baths – an interesting situation reflected in the recent fate of many a large eighteenth century mansion. An alternative possibility is that the southern part of the old Palace was becoming uncongenial, partly through the high water table and partly because once the harbour installations had broken down the area would have reverted to being a marsh with the consequent increase in mosquitoes and other pests. At any event the new baths were built.

The plan was quite simple: the passageway was divided into three by cross partitions. The northern room, the *caldarium*, was fitted with a hypocaust chamber beneath a mortar floor supported on pilae of tiles. The heat was provided by hot air warmed up in a stokery immediately outside the east wall. The masonry sides to the flue still survive, projecting for some 4 ft, showing that they would originally have supported a large boiler of bronze so that the fire would also have heated the water needed by the bathers. Such economy was a common feature in Roman bath-houses.

The middle room, the *tepidarium*, derived its hot air secondhand from the *caldarium* hypocaust and was therefore of a lower temperature. A small plunge bath, just large enough to sit comfortably in, was built in a recess opening from the centre of the west wall. It was floored with tiles and its walls were rendered with a waterproof red mortar. Here in the warm congenial atmosphere the owner and his friends must have spent many a relaxed afternoon.

The third room, to the south, was provided with a central drain made of gutter blocks removed from the old Palace gardens. Since the rest of the details have been destroyed, it is impossible to reconstruct much of the original state of the room, but in all probability it was the cold room (*frigidarium*) where, after some time in the warmth of the other rooms, the pores could be closed with a dousing of cold water before one emerged into the chilling open air. An alternative is that the *frigidarium* was built in the now much ruined room which projected east from the *tepidarium* and that the room with the open drain was a latrine. The evidence is not sufficient to be sure.

The new bath suite was, then, modest but comfortable. Its walls were all carefully plastered and painted with a deep red dado and white panels above, the panels being defined by red bands and outlined with concentric orange frame-lines. Above was a 'cornice moulding' painted in graded tones of red. The window embrasures and doorways were also

32   *The bath suite and exercise hall in the North Wing: early second century*

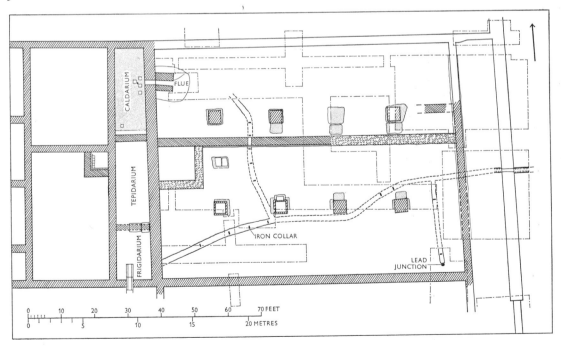

plastered and painted with their angles and splays picked out in red. All three rooms employed this basic decor but the *tepidarium* in addition included some black and yellow areas and panels of white splashed with red and yellow.

The bath suite required an efficient water supply. This was provided by a series of wooden water pipes – lengths of timber hollowed out and jointed together with collars of iron – which were laid in trenches cut through the floor of the aisled hall. The timber has, of course, rotted but it was possible to trace the trenches in which the pipes had been laid and to locate the iron collars used to join the sections. By this means it could be shown that the main pipe led in from the east, twisting between the piers of the hall and ending up in the vicinity of the southern room. Two subsidiary pipes branched off, one running north to the hot water boiler over the *caldarium* flue, the other running to the south-east corner of the hall where it ended with a lead junction box leading to a vertical lead pipe, which would have served a drinking fountain or basin. The way in which the main pipe twisted around the piers suggests that they were still standing at this time, but the northern branch pipe passed neatly through a hole which had been carefully constructed in a new wall built right across the hall from one end to the other on very substantial rubble footings cut through the original floor. The conclusion therefore must be that at the time when the water pipes were laid, or at least were still functioning, the hall was reduced in width from 66 ft to 38 ft, the original southern row of piers now serving as the central supports for the roof of the new structure. The area to the north seems now to have become a working yard from which the flue could be stoked and in which the fuel supply for the baths was housed. The reduction of the hall is interesting because it implies that its original use, as a place of assembly, was now over, the early second-century house no longer needing such a building. Why reconstruction was necessary is not clear, but after 20–30 years the roof timbers may have been beginning to give way under the enormous weight of the roof. The rebuilding was, however, in a good style of masonry and was designed to make maximum use of existing structures and material: the new north wall was probably built entirely from the stone dismantled from the original wall, while the reduced width of the building would allow the original roof timbers to be used even if rotten ends had to be sawn off.

A great deal of trouble had been taken to reconstitute the hall but what function did it now serve? The most reasonable explanation that would fit the few known facts is that it became an exercise hall belonging to the baths. Halls for this purpose were a common adjunct to Roman bathing suites – here one could play games and take exercise before bathing. The small drinking (?) fountain constructed at this time in the corner of the hall would have been an acceptable facility in such an arrangement. As we will see later, the hall may have continued in this function long after the North Wing baths were demolished.

The other late first- or early second-century alterations to the Palace were relatively insignificant structurally but of no less interest. In room N13, in the centre of the North Wing, a remarkable new mosaic was laid over the partly destroyed earlier floor. It was of a complex design consisting of a central roundel enclosing a Medusa head simply drawn in black, red and yellow, with a great mat of hair interwoven with writhing yellow-eyed snakes. The Medusa panel was set in a square surrounded by eight octagonal panels, each enclosing a different type of flower, leaf or rosette. These panels were retained within an overall square frame with the corners filled in with simple chequer-board designs. One of these had been laid incorrectly to have one extra row of squares – this meant that there was not enough room to enclose the adjacent octagon with its correct double border, and even the rosette inside had to be jammed up. This is only one of the numerous small errors which are apparent in the design. The outer borders were composed of multiple bands of different motifs of which the most amusing is of white circles with little pointed tails inside, clearly meant to be a copy of the tendril borders of the West Wing mosaics. The whole floor is extremely lively and crammed with pattern but the technical skill of its mosaicist was low; not only were mistakes made in the basic design but the choice and blend of colours was crude and not at all well thought out. One is forced to the conclusion that it was laid with great enthusiasm by someone with little or no experience, copying what he liked from the mosaics around and making up the rest.

Some indication of the date of the floor is provided by small pieces of samian pottery which had been cut up to form red tesserae used in the main design. Expert opinion has concluded that no piece dating to after AD 90–100 was used. This, as we will see, contrasts noticably with other later mosaics in the building which contain only pottery of mid-second century date. It looks then as though the mosaicist was using pottery currently in use, and that as a method for dating the floors there is some internal consistancy about it. On stylistic grounds and on the basis of the

Plate 32

Fig. 33

samian tesserae, therefore, a date somewhere about or a little before AD 100 is indicated. This is of particular interest because it strongly suggests that we are looking at the first attempt *by local craftsmen* at mosaic art in this country.[32] The earlier mosaics of the Flavian period were all laid by continentals, here surely are the first faltering steps of a local. It is tempting to see in the great profusion of design something of the underlying feeling behind native Celtic art. Perhaps our man was a native artist cashing in on what promised to be a lucrative new medium. Sadly we shall never know.

One other alteration might perhaps belong to this early period, the construction of a corridor along the west side of the North Wing, to link the rooms and corridors of the North Wing to those of the West without one having to go outside the building and use the original colonnades. The new corridor was floored with a simple red tessellated floor with a chequer-board design picked out with grey-brown tesserae. The design is interesting since it incorporates the same ideas as those behind the earlier mosaic in room W 6 – some areas are shown as grey on red, others as red on grey. This simple type of reversal pattern was in use in Italy in the late first and early second centuries but does not seem to have remained in fashion long. The construction of the corridor facilitated the movement between one wing and the other, it also bypassed the north–west corner of the garden which at this time had begun to be used as a tip for kitchen refuse. Its advantages were therefore obvious.

In summary, it may be said that the first series of alterations to the Palace implies that certain important social changes had taken place; the assembly hall was no longer required, the formal garden was beginning to go out of use – both facts strongly suggest that the official-semi-public functions were now at an end. But this does not mean decline, far from it. The bath suite and exercise hall and the new mosaics were expensive luxuries which very few contemporary landowners could afford. Changes there may have been but the quality of domestic life was still very high.

The middle of the second century saw the first major reformation of the old building. The main difficulty in understanding the period is in assessing the order in which the alterations took place and indeed whether they were part of a single cohesive policy of re-building planned at one time, or a series of re-buildings undertaken haphazardly over a period. The archaeological evidence does not allow such fine distinctions to be made but viewing the changes in terms of the overall results it would appear that the builders were working towards a definite preconceived plan.

33 Early second-century mosaic in room N13.
The stippled area has been destroyed by ploughing

The most drastic of the alterations was the demolition of the east end of the North Wing, including the relatively new bath suite. The whole of the superstructure from the west end of the hall to the east end of room N15 was removed down to the footings and the building materials carted off for re-use elsewhere, leaving only loose mortar and chips of stone and tile to be spread out over the old mosaics, several of which miraculously still survived the demolition and were buried. The whole of the colonnaded east courtyard was also pulled down and the rather ragged east end of the North Wing thus exposed was tidied up with a length of wall which created a new corridor and room. There is some evidence to suggest that the old south wall of the wing was retained, linking what was left of the North Wing to the hall.

The reason why these far-reaching demolitions were carried out was simple. The east end of the North Wing had been built over the remains of an early timber building and a number of drainage ditches filled with loose silty soil. Although the Palace footings were substantial enough to remain unaffected, serious subsidence soon began with the result that the colonnades and the floors started to contort and slump. This was no doubt a gradual process but by the middle of the second century, 60 or 70 years after the building was constructed, things had become serious – the subsidence of the mosaic in room N21 shows how bad it was – and the decision to demolish was taken. The demolition meant that the North Wing baths were removed leaving, incidentally, a coin of Hadrian (AD 117–138) in the last lot of ash which they had not bothered to rake out of the flue.

Fig. 34

The replacement baths, built on a larger scale, were inserted into the courtyard of the East Wing, as close as possible to the hall which presumably continued to function as the exercise hall for the bathers. The basis of the new arrangement was fairly simple: the old colonnade was pulled down and a new wall was built right across the courtyard from east to west which, together with the standing walls, created an enclosure 70 ft by 55 ft; within this the baths were built. The old stylobate on the south and east sides of the courtyard was used as the basis for new walls, and a series of cross walls were built dividing up the veranda into two ranges of rooms, into which the baths were inserted. The south range was not used directly for bathing purposes.

Plate 33

The *caldarium* was a small affair, a little under 10 ft square. It was floored in two parts, the northern part was raised on a pillared hypocaust while the southern, at a lower level, was covered with a plain red tessellated

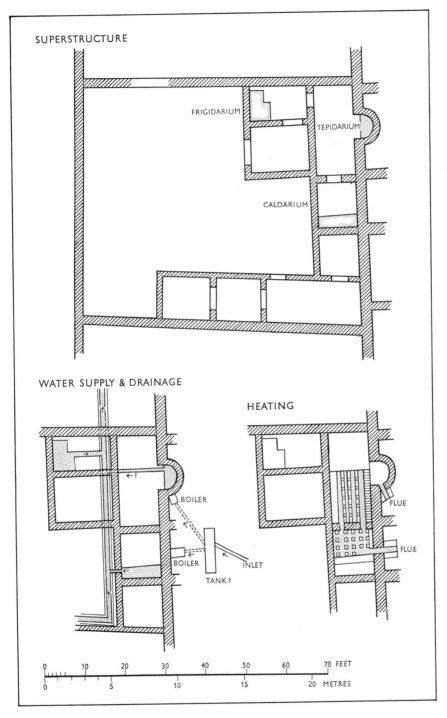

SUPERSTRUCTURE

FRIGIDARIUM

TEPIDARIUM

CALDARIUM

WATER SUPPLY & DRAINAGE

HEATING

BOILER

BOILER

INLET

TANK?

FLUE

FLUE

| | | | | | | | |
0 10 20 30 40 50 60 70 FEET
0 5 10 15 20 METRES

34 *The mid-second-century baths in the East Wing*

floor which sloped to a drain in the west wall. The arrangement is clear enough: the tessellated area was the floor of a hot plunge bath set in the south side of a normally heated *caldarium*. The supply of hot air and water was provided by a stokery outside the east wall, towards which the line of a wooden water pipe could be traced. The water would have been piped into a tank, possibly built on the masonry platform created just east of the flue, and from here it would have been fed, as required, into the hot water boiler – a simple but effective system.

Immediately to the north lay the *tepidarium*, a long room with an apsidal bath built in a recess in its east wall. The heat for the main room was provided by the hot air passing into a series of channels below the floor, linked to the hypocaust of the *caldarium*. Although the sub-floor structures have suffered considerably from robbing, enough survives to show that the arrangement was very carefully thought out. As the plan shows, the air entered through two vents in the dividing wall into two wide channels divided by walls of horizontally set box tiles so that it could pass into the central channels not directly linked to the *caldarium*, thus ensuring an even heat. Along the east wall the box tiles were set closely together and linked to similar tiles set vertically so as to form an internal hollow jacketing to the wall. In this way the hot air, having cir- culated beneath the floor, would have passed into the vertical ducts and would have risen naturally until it was expelled through chimneys set along the top of the wall or in the roof. The small apsidal bath was pro- vided with a subsidiary source of heat by means of a separate stokery, above which would have been its hot water boiler. The waste water from this little bath seems to have passed through a drain set below the floor and then into the old stylobate gutter. This sub-floor drain, though not apparent within the room, marked the north side of the hypocaust system and therefore divided the room into two parts, a southern heated part and a northern cooler section. This type of graded atmosphere is a sophistication seldom met with in small private bathing establishments of this kind.

Plate 63

Next to the *tepidarium* lay the *frigidarium*, a long room with a sunken cold plunge bath in one end. The bath was floored with re-used tiles and slabs of marble set in a hard waterproof cement. In one corner a bench was provided joined to a ledge running along the north wall so that the bathers could sit between plunges with their legs dangling into the water. The benches and the walls of the rooms were coated with a thick layer of waterproof pink mortar. Waste water was removed by means of a

35 *Suggested reconstruction of the mid–second–century baths*

substantial tile-built culvert which ran beneath the floor of the rest of the *frigidarium* and emptied into the stylobate gutter. The arrangement was such that we must suppose the floor of this part of the room was of timber laid above the culvert and the old gutter, no other arrangement was possible under the circumstances.

In the angle between the *caldarium* and the *tepidarium* lay another room with no recognizable internal fittings, which in all probability served as an undressing room (*apodyterium*). In this position it would have been admirably suited for use as a general concourse as well. From here a bather could choose whether to go into the cold plunge or begin his treatment in the more normal way by going into the *tepidarium*, followed by the *caldarium* and finishing of with a cold plunge. Whichever way he chose to use the suite the rooms were conveniently arranged.

The superstructure of the suite can be reconstructed within limits. It is almost certain that the heated rooms were roofed with a vault running north-south from the south wall of the *caldarium* to the north wall of the *tepidarium* – normal architectural procedure would have demanded it and several blocks of tufa, a light stone frequently used in vaults, were found

Fig. 35

179

in the rubble. The *frigidarium* and *apodyterium* were probably protected by a single pitched roof covered with tiles, while the south range may have been given a lean-to roof along the same lines as the original veranda. It is more difficult to say how the old rooms of the East Wing looked by this date, for while the two stokeries built in them would have required some form of roofing to keep off the rain it is most unlikely that much of the original roof remained, not the least because of the problem of ventilation required by the presence of the flues. In all probability much of the roof had been removed; tiles and timber were after all valuable commodities.

Internally, all the walls of the main rooms of the baths were plastered and painted, the best evidence of the general decor coming from the masses of plaster which choked the cold plunge bath. Here, it can be shown, the walls were painted with a deep red dado $3^1/_2$–4 ft high with white walls above divided into panels, each enlivened with a concentric black frameline. The *tepidarium*, however, was far more elaborately decorated with areas painted to represent marble, one in grey splashed with red, black and yellow, another in red splashed with black, both probably serving as part of the dado. Above was some form of elaborate panelling which included bands of bright blue, black and white, but of this upper area little survives.

The drainage system has already been referred to in passing but it deserves a more detailed consideration because of the ingenious way in which the old gutter of the Flavian garden was retained and modified. The three drains from the *caldarium, tepidarium* and cold plunge all lead towards the gutter and must originally have emptied directly into it. The *caldarium* drain was composed of two ceramic water pipes (probably robbed from the garden), placed together so as to form a V-bend, a refinement clearly designed to remove the risk of draughts which would have ruined the comfort of the hot bath. The drain from the much larger cold plunge was necessarily of a more considerable cross section, otherwise it would have taken inordinately long for the bath to empty: since draughts were not a problem here no traps were devised. The third drain, from the *tepidarium*, has been so completely destroyed that nothing can be said of its form. There would, then, have been a considerable volume of water coming from the baths while they were in use, all of it flowing beneath the timber floors of the *frigidarium* and *apodyterium* and into the tile-built culvert through which the waste eventually passed out of the building.

Somewhere in this complex would have been the latrines, placed presumably downstream from the baths themselves. The most likely position for them lies in the recess at the end of the corridor which passed along the north end of the old Flavian east range, exactly over the tile-built culvert. Here, it appears, the sides of the old drain were removed down to its base and two revetting walls were built across so that a sump was formed linked directly to the outfall. Because of one of the revetting walls the water flowing from the baths would have built up behind it and flowed over, flushing out the sump while at the same time the wall prevented a flow-back from the sump towards the baths. Thus by this simple series of alterations an ideal drainage system for a latrine was created. The flooring and seating above, which here would have been constructed in timber, have left no trace and indeed all the surrounding masonry superstructure has been robbed to the footings.

It will be seen from the foregoing description that the new bath suite, built in the middle of the second century to replace the demolished North Wing baths, was well planned, comfortable and rather more spacious than its predecessor. These baths alone suggest a rise in affluence of the owner, a suggestion which is dramatically borne out by the nature of the alterations to the inhabited part of the North Wing.

As we have described above, the eastern part of the North Wing had by the middle of the second century become unsafe through subsidence and was demolished. The western part of the wing, however, continued in active use and it was at about this time that a series of alterations were made to convert the old structure into a more manageable unit. The most necessary alteration was to create an improved system of communications. This was done by adding a new L-shaped corridor to the eastern end of the reconstituted structure and linking it to another corridor made by dividing up room N 14. Thus it was possible to move freely from the east end to the courtyard which was retained as an essential part of the design. At the west end, room N 5 was chopped up into three parts, one was added to room N 4, the original dividing wall now being removed, the second part was floored with a new mosaic pavement and the third became a corridor linking the mosaic room to the tessellated corridor to the west.

It was probably in this phase that a number of the large rooms were divided by timber partitions. Room N 12 was cut into two in this way, the northern part, provided with a new plaster moulding at the junction of the walls and floor, was kept up in style while the southern part eventually became some kind of store room. Rooms N 10 and 11 were also di-

Fig. 36

Plate 55

Plate 56

Plate 53

Plate 57

Plate 62

Plates 46–52

Plate 1

Plate 48

vided by timber walls, both halves of each now being refloored with red tesserae. The southern half of room N11 was also provided with a small patterned mosaic panel. Room N9 on the other hand was retained but refloored with *opus signinum* (a hard mortar containing much crushed brick). The southern part of room N14, of which the northern side was cut off to become a corridor, was refloored with a black and white mosaic very much in the style of the Flavian floor in room N12. While it could have been a direct copy it is more likely that the second-century mosaicist simply relaid, in a rather less competent fashion, the mosaic already there.

The renovated building was now provided with two small heated rooms on either side of room N7, both of which were constructed by dividing off the two corridors, N6 and 8, from the colonnade and cutting them into two almost equal halves. In the northern halves hypocausts were inserted beneath mortar floors, while the hot air needed to heat them was produced by stokeries constructed in the southern halves. This rather peculiar arrangement was necessitated partly by the existing structures into which things had to be fitted, and partly because it seems that the building now fronted north onto the original service road and to have put the flues in the logical place outside the north walls of the rooms would have looked unsightly and ruined the northern approach to the building.

In addition to the purely structural changes, the reconstituted building was provided with four new mosaics, of which the finest was laid in room N7 which now seems to have become the principal room. The patterned panel in the centre of the room was a lively polychrome arrangement in which black and white were dominant but various tones of red and yellow were also used. The centre of the floor, a roundel enclosed within a competently drawn braided guilloche, depicted a winged cupid sitting astride a dolphin and holding its reins in one hand and a trident in the other. While the drawing and shading has a certain lively quality, especially the body muscles which are particularly well conceived, the strange outlining of the figure in black has ruined the effect of the curly hair and has made the hands into rather amorphous shapes. The spacing of the figure within the circle, always a difficult thing to get right, is also unhappy and to deflect the eye from the large area of white in the lower half stylized rocks have been drawn.

The centre roundel is supported within a square panel by four semi-circular panels and four quadrants. The semicircles each contain a fabulous sea beast paired with the one on the opposite side of the floor, two

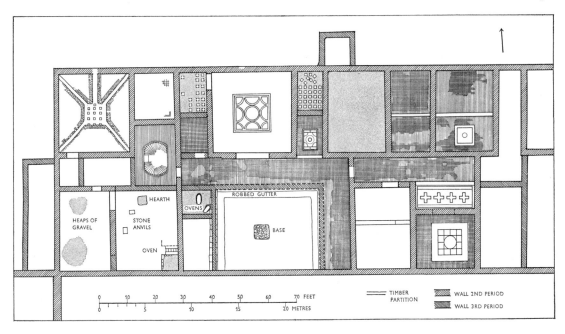

36 The west end of the North Wing, showing all the second- and third-century alterations

being sea panthers and two sea horses. The sea panthers are carefully drawn in yellow, red, black and white, both copying the same basic features but with minor varieties: the western beast has claws and fangs while his partner is of a much more docile appearance. Presumably the difference was deliberately contrived to represent male and female. The two sea horses are predominantly black with details picked out in white and with red tongues. The workmanship of the southern beast is brilliantly assured, the proportions, the stance and the contortions of his tail are all perfectly controlled and result in what must be the most satisfactory piece of design in the whole building. His opposite number is much less happy, a poor emaciated ill-spaced thing, surely the work of a different and less skilled craftsman.

The sea beasts and the shell-like quadrants are retained in simple borders of twisted guilloche. The hollow square spaces between the panels were basically white with large vases in black shown on them. Each vase is different and each has curly handles turning into tendrils and tendrils growing out of the bases – a common technique for filling up awkward spaces.

Plates 51, 52

Plates 46, 47

Plate 49

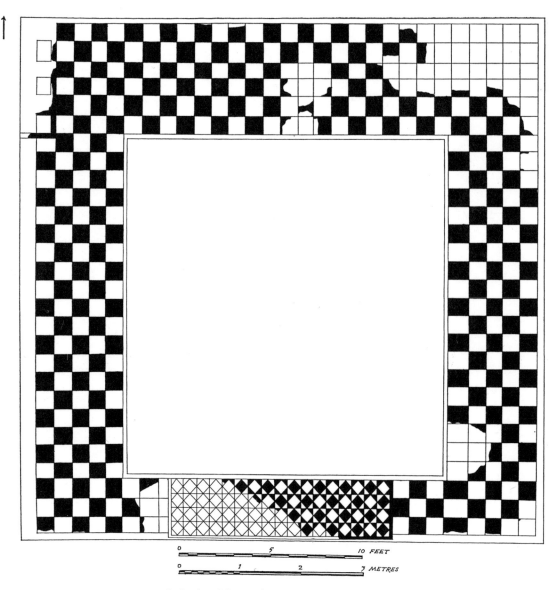

37 *The border of the cupid mosaic in room N7. The central square contains the patterned and figured panel shown in Plate 48*

The design so far described was retained within a square border of twisted guilloche, not without interest for it shows two distinct styles of workmanship, the northern part was rather less ambitious in choice of colour but the mosaicist was good at making the guilloche turn corners. The southern part was more varied in colour range but the corners were incompetently handled. Again, then, we have clear evidence of the work of different people. A further point of interest is that no attempt was made to integrate the guilloche of the enclosed panels with that of the border as was the normal practice later – lack of basic skill, or at least lack of planning, may be the explanation. Outside the guilloche were two further bands of border, one showing triangles arranged base to apex and the outer one depicting central vases supported by simple tendril scrolls. Again an examination of the detail shows both a general lack of fine planning and variations which might well result from the work of different craftsmen. Perhaps the most interesting single detail is on the north side, on the third leaf west from the central vase. Here the mosaicist has twisted the stem in such a way as to leave space for a small black bird. Maybe this is simply a defiant gesture against boredom but another possibility is that it is his signature.

Plate 50

The evidence from the samian tesserae included within the floor suggests a date within the middle part of the second century for its construction. Stylistically this date would be perfectly acceptable, allowing the floor to be placed at the beginning of one of the well defined local schools of craftsmanship, which were growing up in this country as a response to the demands of a society becoming increasingly affluent under Roman rule. While the dolphin floor is a great advance on the Medusa mosaic, it still shows a faltering uncertainty in construction, which incidentally adds enormously to its interest and visual impact.

The patterned panel was set within a surround composed of alternating squares of black and white, another feature harking back to the earlier traditions of the Flavian period. In front of the south side of the floor the pattern becomes more complex, incorporating a square-set-within-square design. This was, in effect, a 'mat', presumably laid to enliven the main entrance to the room, since it ran the full width of the wide south doorway. The door itself was made more impressive by flanking pilasters which can still be traced in the surviving footings. Between these a flight of wooden steps led up from the colonnade to the floor of the room, which was at a higher level. The patterning of the surround also suggests that a door led out of the north-west corner into the little heated room next door.

Fig. 37

The reflooring of the room is most unlikely to have been the only change in decor: in all probability the walls were repainted at the same time. A quantity of wall plaster has been recovered, giving some idea of the fine quality of the work though the individual pieces are too small to allow large-scale reconstruction. The general arrangement was not unlike the Flavian style of inlaid marbles but the quality of the brush-work and choice of colour-range differed. The 'marbles' used included a deep purple with a coarse graining picked out in blue, a pale purple with textures in blue, red and grey, and a dark red backing painted with a curvilinear graining in green and blue. The strip 'marbles' and 'mouldings' were predominantly of black, white and bright blue in various combinations. Another part of the room seems to have been provided with niches painted in white with dangling frills of bright red outlined and enlivened with green. Exactly where in the room this came from we cannot be sure, but one possibility is that the curved plaster does not represent the lining of niches but is, in fact, part of the ceiling painting. Unfortunately there is no way of testing the theory.

It appears, therefore, that the mid-second-century alterations to room N7 were drastic: not only was the interior of the room completely gutted and relined but the main southern entrance was reconstructed with flanking pilasters. Alterations of this style and magnitude imply a considerable expenditure.

The large room in the corner of the wing, room N1, does not appear to have been refloored at this time unless a thin discontinuous lens of mortar which survives represents the basal levels of a mosaic, since removed by the construction of a hypocaust late in the third century. At any event the walls were replastered and painted, as can be shown by the relationship of the base of the painting to a floor level between the original Flavian mosaic and the late third-century hypocaust. A large area of plaster survived in position on the west side of the room, showing that the room was provided with a skirting of deep purple-red followed by a strip of pink painted with purple flowers. Above this was a further horizontal strip in a deep green forming the outermost border of the main wall panels, which here were painted in pale green with designs incorporating pink and white flowers and stripes of other colours. Lying loose in the rubbish of the room were fragments from different designs, including freehand brown and blue painting and areas of yellow splashed with a red-brown. The style is totally different from the Flavian work but there are several similarities, both in the range of colours and the quality of the brushwork, which suggest a close relationship with the more elaborate painting in room N7.

The new room created when N5 was chopped up was no less impressive. It was provided with a fascinating and most unusual mosaic pavement which included a central rectangular element with two apsidal-ended panels, divided into multicoloured rays, attached to each of its long sides. The design is difficult to interpret because a substantial part of the central area has been destroyed, but we believed that it depicted the tails of two fish, the rest of which had been dug away by a later pit. If this were so then the semicircular rayed panels were probably scallop shells like the famous mosaic depicting a large shell found in the Roman town of Verulamium (St Albans).[33] For a long time we referred to the floor as the shell mosaic. During the preparation for opening the site to the public, however, while the team of Italian mosaicists were consolidating the mosaic by regrouting it, we became aware that they were calling it the Peacock floor: the reason was soon apparent. Viewed from the west the two 'fish tails' look very much like the knobbly legs of a bird, the 'tails' being the feet and what was considered to be a fin could well be a spur. If this is so then the 'shells' can be envisaged as the opened up tail of a peacock. It is still difficult to be sure which interpretation is correct. The peacock explanation is rather more attractive but unless a similar floor is found elsewhere we will never know.

Plate 55

Room N2, to the north, was provided with a mosaic pavement at this stage but very little survives except for the edge of a panel and a chequerboard pattern of black and white squares. The other rooms at the west end of the North Wing all retained their original Flavian mosaics, which continued to be heavily used and patched whenever holes appeared.

The fourth mosaic assignable to the middle of the second century was laid in the southern half of the divided room N8, as a small multi-coloured panel in the middle of a plain red tessellated floor. It consisted quite simply of a central rosette surrounded by a complex and rather inconsistent fret pattern which in turn was enclosed within a border of coloured cushion-shaped lenses arranged diagonally. Although the floor was simple and unassuming it would have provided a centre of interest in the room, suggesting it may have served as an ante-room to its northern half where furniture and fittings would have relieved the need for patterned floors.

Plate 57

In the south-west corner of the wing rooms N3 and the enlarged N4 appear to have been used as work rooms and perhaps for storage, but whether this began in the second century or later cannot be determined. Room N4 was fitted with a substantial oven inserted into the south-east corner and represented now only by its flue, but the basic structure was of considerable proportions and it could well have served as the bakery replacing the isolated Flavian bakery which had gone out of use by the early second century. A small hearth was built in the northern part of the

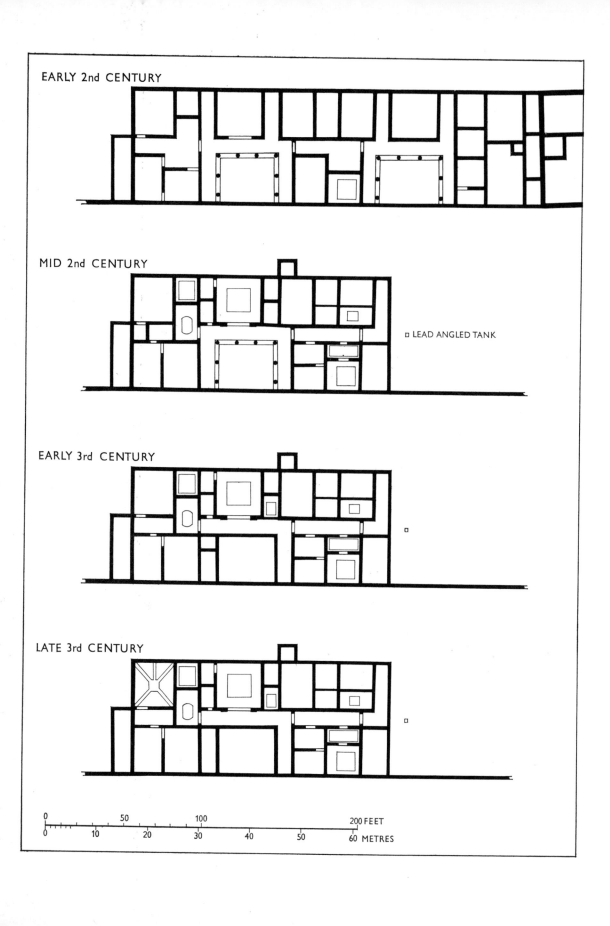

EARLY 2nd CENTURY

MID 2nd CENTURY

□ LEAD ANGLED TANK

EARLY 3rd CENTURY

LATE 3rd CENTURY

| 0 | 50 | 100 | 200 FEET |
| 0 | 10 | 20 | 30 | 40 | 50 | 60 METRES |

room at about this time, but no particular function can be assigned to it. Finally two large blocks of stone were found on the floor with their upper surfaces very worn as the result of a pounding or hammering process.

An examination of the immediate environment of the reconstituted North Wing shows that to the west, south-west and east, thick layers of black occupation rubbish began to accumulate. This does not necessarily imply that middens were allowed to form close to the building, such squalor would hardly have been allowed at the time when the building was so rapidly developing. It is far more reasonable to interpret this material as the direct result of the deliberate manuring of gardens around the building with kitchen refuse. The abraded nature of the potsherds tends to support the view that the ground had been well dug over. Immediately outside the new east end of the wing a wooden tank about 18 ins square had been set into the ground; while the wood has rotted the internal angle bindings of lead and the large-headed iron tacks which held them in place still survived in position. It is now impossible to define the function of the tank.

The north side of the building was, as we have mentioned above, its front, looking out upon the Flavian enclosure, a made-up area crossed by a metalled road linked directly to the north-south service road. At least one forward projecting addition was made to the building at this time, attached to the north wall of room N9, but its function is unclear unless it served as a porch. The area around it had been metalled with compacted gravel in a manner suitable for an entrance path. The excavation of this area has been only limited and further details are at present lacking.

During the first fifty years of the second century the old palace was altered out of all recognition. From a vast semi-public residence set in splendid landscaped surroundings it was transformed into a smaller, and no doubt far more comfortable, villa concentrated in the west part of the North Wing with a detached bath suite inserted into the old East Wing. How much demolition of obsolete structures took place during this time it is impossible to say. Parts of the North and East Wings were certainly *Fig. 38* razed but, as we will see in the next chapter, much of the West Wing probably remained in a roofed state, and for a while the old entrance hall continued to be used. Of the southern part of the Palace we are entirely ignorant. The complete absence of second- and third-century finds from the admittedly limited excavation might suggest that this part of the site was no longer occupied but it would be unwise to argue solely from the absence of evidence. One interesting detail is that a fence was constructed at some post-Flavian date across the garden more or less along the line of the north side of the central path, some of the posts cutting into the now disused bedding trenches. The fence is otherwise undated but its close relationship to the axis of the building suggests a Roman date. It could be the southern boundary fence of the second-century building dividing the occupied area from the abandoned and demolished southern side.

While it is true to say that the building had been drastically reduced in size and strictly can no longer be considered as a palace, the standard of living was still remarkably high. Its owners were not living in a parasitic fashion on the luxuries of the past, they had virtually constructed within the shell of the old structure a completely new villa geared to a smaller establishment of staff and to the domestic needs of a single family, but they had done so in a style still exceptional in the contemporary countryside. Extremely few second, or even early third, century villas could boast four new polychrome mosaics and a bath suite. The mere fact that the baths could be totally rebuilt within fifty years is a measure of the wealth available. Who the second-century owners were we will never know – perhaps they were the family of the old king who now, with no official status, were unable to keep up the standards of the past. Alternatively the estates may have been sold off to wealthy locals. It is one of the many intriguing questions which must remain unanswered.

X

The Third Century

Throughout most of the third century the inhabited part of the North Wing was subjected to changes, usually of a relatively minor nature, which maintained and improved slightly the standard of living without dramatically altering it. To begin with the little hypocaust rooms on either side of room N7 proved awkward to work: the flues would have belched smoke into the rest of the building and supplies of fuel had to be carried into the centre of the inhabited structure. Clearly this was all highly unsatisfactory. Early in the third century therefore they ceased to be heated and the southern parts of the elongated passage which had housed the stokeries were levelled up and new floors were laid, a plain red tessellated floor in room N6 and a small mosaic surrounded by a tessellated border in N8. The re-flooring in room N6 was particularly interesting because beneath it, in the ash and rubble levelled up to form its foundation, a silver denarius of the Emperor Septimius Severus was found. The coin was of a type issued in 196–7 and since it was only slightly worn it cannot have been in circulation for long. The floor above it is therefore unlikely to date much after the early years of the third century. The mosaic in room N8, which in all probability is part of the same series of alterations, may therefore be of about the same date.

The mosaic is of an interesting but straightforward design. In the centre is a complex knot motif enclosed within a circle of braided guilloche which floats on a plain white background supported on four sides by pairs of dolphins facing centrally-placed vases. All this is set within a square frame, with shell motifs in the corners, and with additional panels containing diamonds at each end. The room seems to have been divided by a timber partition from the veranda to the south. The floor is too simple to enable much to be said of its stylistic affinities except that an early third-century date would be acceptable. Its interest lies mainly in the relative sterility of the competently executed pattern. The mosaicists available in the early third century at Fishbourne were not as able as those practising half a century earlier.

Plate 54

Plate 61

At the time of these refloorings alterations were made to the courtyard immediately to the south. Until then it seems that the original colonnade had been retained with its gutter still functioning to carry off the rain-water. Now, however, the columns were removed and their place taken along the north and east sides by dwarf walls, probably with some kind of balustrade supporting the veranda roof. The north and east sides of the veranda were then floored with red tessellation. Although the dwarf wall and the original stylobate blocks upon which it was built have been robbed away, much of the tessellated floor remains in position at such a level that the wall must have been built to revet its outer edge, otherwise the stylobate blocks would have been too low. The veranda floor can be shown to be of early third-century date because it was laid in one with the tessellated surround to the mosaic in room N 8. The improvement to the courtyard, which really amounted to partially closing it in, was a logical follow-up to the abandonment of the stokeries: the whole of this south side was now linked closely together as a single unit.

At this time the western arm of the veranda was completely walled in to form a pair of work rooms, one of which was provided with a small oven. This new unit, together with the rooms to the west, N 3 and 4, comprised the work rooms and kitchens of the building which were neatly tucked away in one corner, the rest of the inhabited part of the building forming an L-shape.

The reconstruction of the veranda tended to turn it into a linking corridor as opposed to a place from which the enclosed garden could be viewed, the old garden now serving more as a light-well than an integral part of the landscaping. It is probably at about this time that a massive concrete foundation was laid within the garden, measuring about 6 ft square and nearly 2 ft deep, and built of layers of greensand rubble interleaved with thick spreads of pink mortar. The top of the foundation, which was level with the surface of the ground, was set with tiles showing some signs of wear. What manner of structure would have required so massive a foundation it is difficult to say, but it can hardly have been a garden ornament. It is more likely to have supported a domestic feature, perhaps the base for a handmill or even a press of some kind, in which case the old garden had become part of the working area. There is certainly a neat logic behind these late modifications.

Nothing has yet been said of the fate of the West Wing during the second and third centuries largely because, while alterations to the original structure can be recognized, they cannot be dated. Within the rooms of the wing the observable changes were slight. The awkwardly shaped room W 3 was divided by a wall laid directly on the original mosaic (thus incidentally preserving a wide strip from later destruction) and in room W 6, immediately to the south, the worn mosaic floor was patched with red tesserae while some form of projecting plinth was built out from the wall. These are the only surviving alterations, but it must be admitted that the Saxon and medieval ploughing which has so destroyed the mosaic floors would also have carried away all trace of any superficial late partition walls.

In the old East Wing the bath suite continued to function with no major alteration or refitting throughout the third century, but there is evidence to show that the easternmost wall of the building had been demolished to its footings and in all probability the roofs of the east range had long since been removed. There is no trace of any form of occupation, rebuilding or reflooring within the rooms after the Flavian period, with the exception of the small late hearth in room E 2. Apart from this the only structure of post-Flavian date to survive, other than the baths, is a well dug close to the north wall of the entrance hall in the south-east corner of the small courtyard. First of all a pit about 6^1/$_2$ ft across and 7 ft deep had been dug down to the water-bearing gravel and within this a box-like timber structure was built up using rough oak timbers placed in pairs, each successive layer at right angles to the one below. Between the timbers and the side of the well pit, tips of rubble and gravel were thrown in, including part of a tile-built arch from a destroyed building, to serve as a filter for the muddy water percolating in from the surrounding soil. Timber unfortunately rots rapidly under normal conditions, due largely to the action of aerobic bacteria – that is bacteria which require air to live – but when timbers are completely immersed in water and do not dry out, bacterial action is prevented and the timbers are preserved. This was so in the case of the lowest two pairs of well timbers, which had always been below water and therefore survived: above them all trace of the upper framing had completely disappeared. Some time during the late second or early third century the well was abandoned and filled with rubbish of various kinds including pottery, part of a basin of Purbeck marble and a large section of a base belonging to a column. The column had fractured during use and had to be clamped together with iron ties. A flake had also fallen off the shaft and had been carefully pegged back in place with square dowels. The siting of the well is particularly interesting because it was dug exactly over the bed of the old stream filled in in the

Plates 64, 65

60's of the first century. Either its course had been divined or, more likely, the subsidence of the surrounding structures gave it away, always supposing that the siting was not purely accidental.

Whatever happened to the southern part of the Palace in the second and third centuries, it is clear that the entrance hall continued to stand for most of the time, although the marble lining from the pool would have been one of the first things to be taken away. At an early stage the colonnaded fronts to the hall were removed and excavation has shown how the gravel of the street gradually washed over the exposed footings right up to the front entrance, now allowing access to vehicles as well as pedestrians. Columns of this size would have been a valuable commodity for which Chichester would have provided a ready market. But in spite of this the walls and roofs remained. Traffic through the hall was heavy and soon wore away the mortar floor. To begin with attempts were made to patch it but eventually they ceased and the vehicles and feet cut deeply into the clay make-up beneath. After a while the volume of traffic lessened sufficiently to allow a layer of turf to form over the northern part of the hall, but pedestrians and carts still hugged the south wall. Then the roof fell in: the old rafters finally gave way and masses of tiles collapsed onto the floor. Complete tiles, if there were any left by this time, would have been carried away, leaving the rest of the fragments where they had fallen to be trampled under foot. The tiles show very clearly how the traffic funnelled between the piers of the western bay, wearing smooth the fragments lying in the main path but leaving those close against the walls and piers freshly broken and untrampled. Where all this traffic was going is not immediately apparent. It was evidently turning off the road into or across the area of the Flavian garden. If the South Wing had been demolished at an early date, a track might well have led down to the harbour, but positive evidence is not available.

Towards the end of the century it is possible to detect signs of incipient change, giving the impression that a new building programme was underway. This comes out most clearly in the room N1 in the extreme north-west corner of the North Wing, where work had begun on the construction of a new hypocaust system. Instead of digging out the hypocaust chambers below the existing floor level, the new installations were constructed on the floor, the intention being to create a new level some 2–3 ft above it. In the centre of the room the main hypocaust chamber, measuring about 8 ft square, was constructed of a floor of upturned roof tiles with side walls built of greensand blocks and bonding courses of tiles set

Plates 58–60

in clay. On the floor were erected thirteen pilae composed of broken tiles which were to support the raised floor. Into the north side of the chamber opened the hot air inlet, a wide channel covered with overlapping roof tiles. The recurring use of roof tiles, which were probably expensive to produce and were certainly unsuitable for the purpose of general building, is interesting. It tends to suggest that the builders had at their disposal a quantity of secondhand tiles, salvaged perhaps from some other part of the building, and used these rather than going to the expense of buying new bricks. The corners of the chamber were joined by channels running diagonally to the corners of the room where they would have met vertical vents set in the walls. This kind of arrangement worked very efficiently, for the hot air, once it had been forced into the central chamber from the stokery, would have passed into the diagonal channels and thence to the vertical vents where it would have tended naturally to rise. Once the circulation had begun it would have continued, hot air being drawn in as the draughts were created by the efficient functioning of the vents and their chimneys. Experiments elsewhere have shown that constant stoking was not necessary – as soon as the required temperature was reached stoking ceased and the room remained hot for a considerable time by virtue of the heat which the surrounding masonry had absorbed. In fact this kind of Roman hypocaust embodies the same principles as modern night-storage heaters.

This, then, is the system which the builders intended to insert into the room. They had got as far as constructing the foundation works and had begun to fill in the spaces between the channels with rubble when building ceased. Two pieces of evidence allow this conclusion to be reached: first, a careful examination of the mouth of the flue showed that the tiles and the clay in which they had been set bore no discolouration as they would have done had they been subjected to heat, nor was there any ash or charcoal in the channel. Second, there was no trace of a broken-up floor in the chamber beneath the centre of the room. Together the facts show that the system was never fired and that in all probability the floor had never been laid – we are looking at a piece of unfinished work.

Some further light was thrown on the situation by the discovery, in room N3 to the south, of two large heaps of a coarse gritty mortar mixed up ready for use and actually retained by planks to prevent it spilling too far. This must have been the mortar intended for the floor above the hypocaust, but it was never used.

There are other, less impressive, signs of activity at this time. In the West Wing, for example, the mosaic in room W 3 was being uprooted, tesserae were shovelled into heaps in the corner of the room where they still lay 1,600 years later, but many sack-loads must have been carried off, perhaps for temporary storage in the old aisled hall where a large heap of loose stones was found. They may have represented raw material waiting for the mosaicist who was to lay a new floor above the hypocaust. Finally, in room N 11, a substantial heap of window panes had been amassed; they were stacked on the floor in the corner of the room ready to be used again when the reconstruction had reached a sufficiently advanced stage.

Other minor works were undertaken at this time or a little earlier, the partition wall across the passage between rooms N 1 and 3 was removed, presumably facilitating movement between the two rooms, which would have helped the efficiency of the building programme. The partition between the two rooms of the kitchen, built into the east veranda of the corridor, was also pulled down. Both compartments were then refloored together and a new oven, showing little sign of use, was built.

There are, then, signs that building work was in progress towards the end of the third century. What was in the minds of the owners it is impossible now to say, but one room was clearly being fitted out with an expensive system of under-floor heating and it may be that more extensive alterations were about to be undertaken, using up stock-piles of tesserae, window panes, roof tiles and probably timbers derived from the demolition of now defunct pieces of the old building. After all, the building was virtually an antique, 200 years old, that had not been brought up to date for at least 80 years. It is no wonder that a little modernization was being carried out. In the Province generally the late third and early fourth century was a time of massive rebuilding, particularly in the countryside. It was now that the great country mansions were beginning to reach their most developed form. Indeed there was sufficient work available for schools of mosaicists to become established in many of the main urban centres. Perhaps the owners of Fishbourne were ready for a large-scale rebuilding to bring the old villa right up to date, but this was never to be, for a disastrous fire destroyed everything.

73 Room N 12 in the North Wing, showing a mass of broken pottery which had been standing on a table or shelf at the time of the disastrous late third-century fire. The pottery had been crushed and discoloured by the weight of the burning rafters falling on it

74 In another part of the same room puddles of lead were found on the floor amid groups of iron fittings. The lead would have been used in the roof and when the fire took hold, melted and dropped on to the floor

< 75, 76 *Opposite, above,* puddles of lead lying on a corridor floor. The absence of brick tesserae beneath the lead shows that the floor was wearing out at the time of the fire. *Below,* one of the door sills in the North Wing, burnt at the time of the fire

77 The stylobate and gutter blocks of the old palace provided a valuable source of building stone after the building ceased to be inhabited. The gutter blocks of the East Wing courtyard can be seen here, dragged from their original positions ready for removal

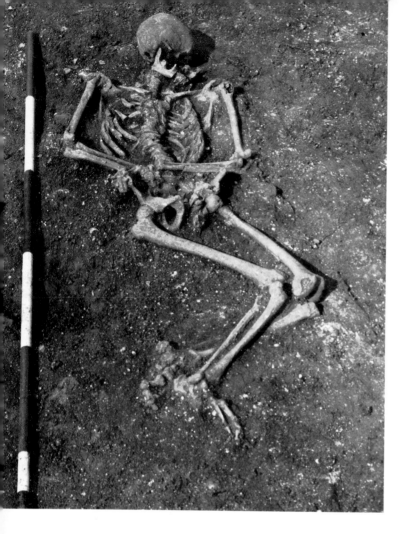

78, 79 After the building had been totally demolished the site was used, in a limited way, as a burial ground. The exact date of the interments is unknown, but they may well be of the fifth century

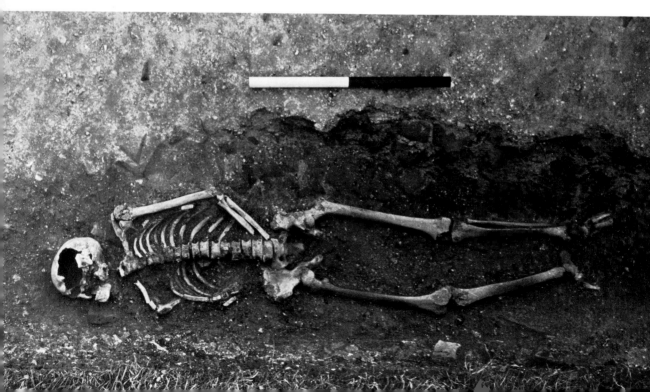

80 The eastern wall of the palace was provided with small arched openings in the footings below ground-level. They were probably built to allow ground water to percolate into a rubble drain, thus preventing the building-up of water-pressure

81, 82　An iron padlock and a length of chain found on the floor of room N 12, sealed by the layer of burnt rafters. Elaborate padlocks of this kind are rare in Roman Britain

83　From the waterlogged deposits > found by trial trenching in the Roman harbour, south of the palace, came large quantities of domestic rubbish including a wooden bowl (centre), and fragments of leather shoes and boots, together with twigs and fir-cones

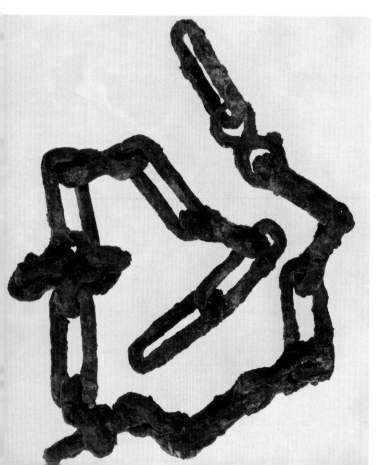

84　Three 'hippo-sandals' found to- > gether with the padlock and chain on the floor of room N 12. Their exact function is in dispute, but they are generally thought to have been temporary shoes for beasts of burden

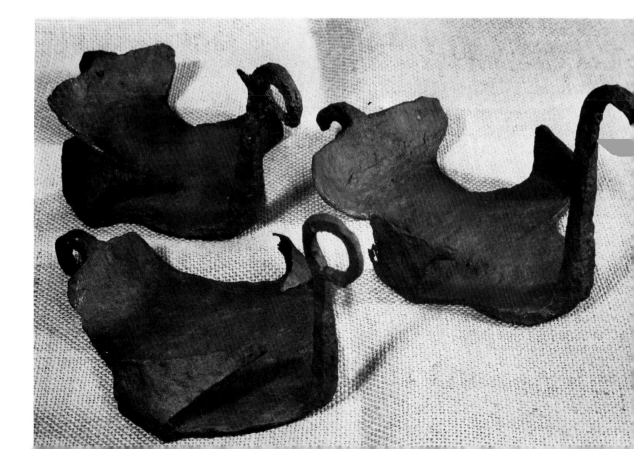

85, 86 The opening of the palace to the public was preceded by a considerable programme of conservation. *Above*, fragments of fallen wall plaster are replaced in position; *below*, a mosaic floor is seen during the relaying operation

XI

Everyday Life

We do not, in this chapter, attempt to describe the daily life of the Palace which, indeed, it would be impossible to do, nor is this an account of Romano-British life in general for there are several good books on the subject to which Fishbourne has little to add.[34] Instead, what is attempted here is a description of certain aspects of the non-architectural situation at Fishbourne which can be seen through the objects recovered from the excavations.

The excavation of any Roman habitation site on the scale of the Fishbourne dig would invariably discover enormous quantities of occupation rubbish, principally broken pottery and animal bones as well as numbers of the trinkets commonly in use during the Roman occupation. Fishbourne was no exception. More than two thousand individual objects have been recovered, ranging from fragments of broken pins to part of a marble sculptured head, together with many hundreds of boxes of broken pottery and animal bones. Any account offered here must necessarily be a summary, thus the emphasis will tend to be on the more unusual objects rather than those which commonly occur on most sites.

The furniture of the Palace must have been as exceptional as the building itself, but so little of it survives under normal archaeological conditions that we can have no true idea of its quality. There must have been many statues scattered around the Palace and its gardens, but art objects of marble and bronze were valuable commodities which would have found a ready market in the later periods of the Palace's decline. Of bronze statues all that survive are a few scraps of cast metal, one piece showing signs of having been gilded.

The marble statuary is better represented by the remarkable discovery of part of the head of a child, which had been thrown away with tips of rubble into one of the robber trenches created when the walls of the North Wing were being demolished. The head is a life-size representation, carved from a white crystalline marble from Italy, in a style which is strongly suggestive of late first-century work. The facial characteristics are clearly those of a particular individual rather than a generalized deity,

Plate 66

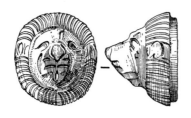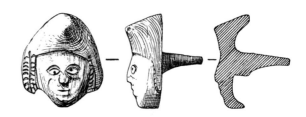

39 *Decorated bronze terminals (actual size)*

but no match can be found among the members of the Imperial household. Perhaps we are looking at a child of the owner's family, a boy with a sulky pouting mouth, generally rather fat and with somewhat protruding ears. The top of his head has been cut away diagonally and the centre shows signs of an iron dowel, implying either that he was part of a group, possibly with a hand of an elder resting on his head or, far more likely, that he had once been provided with a separate helmet made in metal. This single fragment provides a tantalizing glimpse not only of the extremely high quality of the statuary with which the Palace was adorned, but also perhaps of the facial characteristics of someone who may even have been the owner's son.

Under the general heading of furniture would come all the wooden, leather and wicker fittings which stand no chance of survival under normal archaeological conditions. However, the furniture inlay cut out of coloured stones in the masons' working yard hints at the presence of elaborately inlaid table tops. One fragment, of a beautifully designed leaf, from the general rubble of the North Wing, implies some far more elaborate designs than those incorporating the more commonly occurring geometric shapes. Other articles of furniture were decorated with bronze studs, some quite plain, the others with elaborately cast and incised terminals. One bears a representation of a lion's head partly moulded, partly incised; another has the face of a man wearing a Phrygian cap. It, too, is largely moulded but the features are picked out with incisions. Both can be paralleled on other sites in Britain and were probably mass-produced in a single workshop making whatever article of furniture they once adorned. Another object of some quality is a bronze handle belonging perhaps to a drawer or box, cast in the form of two dolphins arranged nose to nose, their tails providing convenient points of attachment for the rings by which they were joined to the wood. Here again limited incision is used to enliven certain features, particularly the eyes. A wide range of other fittings of various kinds, mainly in bronze, have been found which

Plate v
Fig. 39

Fig. 40

206

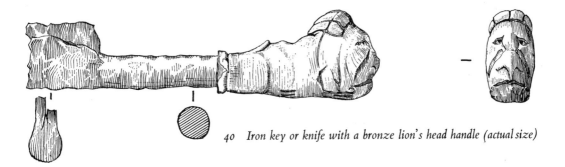

40   Iron key or knife with a bronze lion's head handle (actual size)

probably come from furniture of some kind. Similarly, the various small keys and parts of locks in bronze were fine enough to have belonged to chests and cupboards.

Personal dress is rather easier to assess from archaeological evidence. Shoes were widely worn – the impressions of hobnail boots and sandals made on tiles while they were laid out to dry show that, wherever the tiles were made, feet were more frequently shod than not. Fragments of the leather shoes themselves have begun to appear in the waterlogged levels filling the harbour. So far pieces of heels, insteps and uppers have been recovered and much more remains there to be found. Apart from a piece of leather jerkin from the harbour, no direct evidence of the clothes themselves survives, but one might expect the toga to have been popular, particularly after the Flavian Palace had been built. The fact that very few of the brooches recovered date to the Flavian period or later might be thought to support the idea that the toga ousted simpler kinds of dress requiring brooches (*fibulae*) to hold the folds together. One interesting object, a dress fastener, was recovered from the early levels. It is simply a decorated ring of bronze attached to a shank, which would have been sewn to cloth or leather. The ring could then be slipped through a hole cut into the other side of the garment. In fact the arrangement is very close to the modern button and buttonhole. The head of this particular dress fastener was enlivened with simple inset circles of different coloured enamels in a Celtic fashion, a point which serves to remind us that dress fasteners are thought to derive from the north of England, probably in-fluenced by strong native traditions. Here, then, is some evidence to sug-gest the presence of people dressed in native costume.

Large pins to fasten clothes and keep the hair in place commonly oc-curred in all levels, almost invariably made of bone. Only one example was found made from the far more valuable jet, a hard black stone sup-posedly endowed with magical properties, mined in Yorkshire. Crude jet seems to have been taken to York for manufacture into pins, armlets

Plate 83

and medallions, and the finished objects exported from there. The Fishbourne pin, with its finely carved vase-shaped head is identical to one found with a burial outside York.

Bracelets occurred in great numbers, some made from Kimmeridge shale quarried in Dorset, others from bronze either twisted into rope-like form or cut and stamped out of sheets of metal. None were particularly outstanding. The one earring found was, however, more exotic. The surviving part consisted simply of an oval box-like setting of gold, with a flange around it, inset with a green glass paste. It was probably the setting from what we would now call a drop-earring. It was mislaid one day by a lady strolling in the Palace garden – she may have been unable to find it among the bushes or perhaps she was unaware even that she had lost it, we will never know.

Plate 67

Finger-rings were popular. Most of them were of bronze, but one silver ring was found, belonging to a child: it had been engraved with a small bird on the bezel. A second child's ring was of gold, inset with an oval intaglio of dark green plasma again engraved with a bird. Gold rings are a distinct rarity in Britain in the first century, for at this time to be allowed to wear such a ring was a privilege restricted to those who were born free and owned sufficient money and property to make them eligible to belong to the Equestrian Order or be of senatorial rank. Should a man have attained this rank, his wife and children were also allowed to wear gold rings. This particular ring was found in a level dating to the time when the proto-palace was in use. Its discovery therefore tends to support the view that the building belonged to a man of exceptionally high rank.

The intaglios from two other rings have been recovered. The first is in green glass with a moulded crow or raven on it, enclosed within a raised flange. The raven is a popular bird in Roman folk tradition. It is a bird of prophecy thought to herald prosperity and would therefore probably be thought of as a lucky charm. The second gem is far more exotic. It is an oval amethyst nearly half an inch long engraved with an almost naked Mercury leaning against a pillar; he wears a short cape and a broad-brimmed hat sprouting wings and carries a money-bag in one hand and a staff, called a caduceus, in the other. At his feet are engraved two of the animals commonly associated with him: a cock and a ram: the cock to represent the god's wakefulness and the ram as a reminder of his patronage of flocks and herds. The craftsmanship and finish of the intaglio are superb; there can be no doubt that it was a most valuable possession closely guarded, the loss of which must have been catastrophic. It was found in the entrance hall of the Flavian Palace where it might have been dropped by someone, in the late first or early second century, who was perhaps only visiting. By a remarkable coincidence the elder Pliny wrote in his *Natural Histories*, that 'the Magi ... assert that amethysts will assist people who are about to approach a king as suppliants'.[35] His concluding statement that 'they keep off hail and locusts' seems to be rather less relevant in the present context.

Brooches, bracelets, earrings and rings are all evocative of the finery of life at the Palace, but there are other aspects that are represented less directly in the archaeological record. Cosmetics, for example, are hinted at by the finely finished stone palettes upon which they would have been mixed, by the small scent bottles and by the spatulae which served to extract creams and ointments from long-necked bottles. For general purposes of preening themselves the ladies used toilet sets of tweezers, nail cleaners and the instruments often inelegantly referred to as ear-scoops. Nor must we forget the gaily coloured cloths, the braids and perhaps the silks which might have been worn. All these are aspects of the sophisticated life which must have been played out within the Palace in its *floruit*. The only hope of being able to discover more details of these less tangible sides of life lie, incongruously enough, in the mud and slime of the harbour where organic traces tend to be well preserved.

The well-dressed inhabitants would have been equally well fed. The artifacts of food preparation are plentiful on most archaeological sites and Fishbourne is no exception. We have already mentioned milling, baking and the problems of food storage. Meat was plentiful particularly from the three basic farmyard animals of sheep, ox and pig. Pig, a favourite animal in the preceding Iron Age and one to which the woodland hereabouts was particularly suited, was prominent in the earlier periods but was gradually replaced as time went on by beef and mutton, bought no doubt in the local markets or reared on the estate. Hunting seems to have been of very little importance; even wild boar which one might have expected to be abundant, was represented by only one animal. Fishing was certainly practised, as the bronze barbed fishhook, netting needles and net-weights show, and wild birds from the marshes were trapped or shot. At one stage a surprisingly wide variety of straggly hens were in residence, providing meat and eggs while their cocks, with well developed fighting spurs, would have offered sport.

In addition to these basic homegrown commodities, much would have been imported. Olive oil, olives and wine would have been brought to the harbour in large storage vessels, amphorae, which were often stamped with the maker's name, enabling their place of origin to be identified. The limited excavation of the harbour area so far carried out has produced a very large quantity of amphorae fragments, perhaps from containers broken on unloading and swept overboard. Other things such as exotic spices and herbs not available in this country would have been imported, possibly in pottery containers. A number of unusual fancy vessels have been found which were more likely to have been brought to this country for their contents than for their intrinsic interest. One of these, a jug from the Loire region of France, was ornamented with an applied roundel stamped with a scene depicting gladiators. Whilst common in parts of France they are virtually unknown elsewhere in Britain.

Plate 68

Shellfish were eaten in quantity on Roman sites and were readily available fresh to those who were fortunate enough to live near the coasts. All the harbours hereabouts could have grown oysters in vast numbers, indeed they did so until well into the last century when pollution became so great that the oyster population died off. Other shellfish less commonly found include mussels, cockles, winkles and scallops. Served in quantity they were common food rather than the delicacy they are today.

A number of foodstuffs, particularly fresh vegetables, would have been grown in the kitchen gardens.[36] There were, of course, no potatoes but varieties of cabbage were common. The writer Columella describes fifteen different types which include cabbage itself, lettuce, sprouts and cauliflower. In addition to being good to eat, vegetables were regarded as possessing medicinal value. The cabbage, Pliny the Elder tells us, was good for 87 different cures. Lentils, peas and beans were grown, together with all types of root crops including varieties of onions, radishes, carrots, parsnips, turnips, as well as vegetables such as cucumber and asparagus. The only one of these to leave any archaeological trace at Fishbourne is the lentil of which a jar full was found in a store room in the North Wing. There can be little doubt, however, that the Flavian Palace was provided with a well stocked kitchen garden in which most of the common vegetables would have been produced.

The only source of sweetness in the Roman world was honey, and beekeeping was reduced to a fine art. It is now generally believed that some of the very large pottery vessels, which have been classified under the general heading of storage jars, were in fact ceramic beehives. There is one type, of which fragments have been found at Fishbourne, with small perforations in the body and base which would have served admirably, the holes providing the necessary ventilation for the bees. Salt, too, was an important commodity, but it presented no problem at Fishbourne, for there were extensive salt pans around the fringes of the neighbouring harbours where, by a process of natural and artificial evaporation, the salt could be extracted from sea water.

The preparation of the food is far more difficult to describe from the surviving archaeological fragments, but we have already seen something of the bread baking process (p. 146). Vegetables were ground up in mortars, either small basins of Purbeck marble or the far more common ceramic mortaria made in specialized factories in this country and abroad, tough enough to take a considerable pounding. The mortaria were provided with pouring lips so that liquid could be poured off and possibly strained through ceramic strainers. Cooking, usually on a gridiron over an open fire, was carried out using large vessels capable of holding on average between 2 and 4 pints. The discoloured sherds of these cooking pots are a common feature of the rubbish deposits – the breakage rate must have been high. In addition to the pots there were saucepans or skillets of bronze, a few fragments of which have been found.

The food would have been served in a wide range of dishes and plates, the best being the well finished, but mass-produced, imports known as samian ware, a glossy red pottery produced in factories in Gaul and imported in vast amounts into this country. Fine imported glassware, some of it multicoloured, some cut, also seems to have been used in quantity.

The administration of so large and complex an estate must have required an advanced form of book-keeping and necessarily implies a high degree of literacy. Again there is some archaeological evidence of this. In the early levels glass counters and small pebbles for calculating are found in large numbers (our word 'calculate' came from the Latin *calculus*, meaning a pebble). By the time that the Flavian Palace was being erected records were written in Latin, as part of a tally found inscribed on a column drum reminds us. It records three names with quantities at the side, presumably referring to some kind of work carried out at the time when the Palace was built. Names were also scratched on pots, possibly by their owners. That writing was fairly widely practised is shown by the discovery of several ink wells as well as stylae for writing on wax tablets, and even a bronze stylus-case. Letters and packages were also being prepared and sealed by drawing the strings into a wax-filled seal box of bronze. A number of these have been found from various levels, particularly in and after the Flavian period. There can be little doubt that

Plate 69

the Palace staff must have included scribes and record keepers simply to maintain the complex organization. It is more difficult to say whether the evidence for writing necessarily implies a regard for literature by the owner's family. Here again the only hope of discovering papyrus or writing tablets is when the waterlogged deposits of the harbour are more fully examined.

Finally, what can be said of the religious practices of the inhabitants? Apart from the aisled hall which may have served a religious function as well as being a place of assembly, no other religious structures can be recognized, unless the tiled base in front of the audience chamber was for an altar rather than a statue. Among the small objects recovered there are only two which have religious associations: a small bone amulet carved with a clenched fist at one end and a phallus at the other, and a fragment of a figured pottery vessel. The amulet is of a fairly common type which would have been worn round the neck to ward off evil. The vessel is, however, far more unusual. When complete it would have been of jug-like form decorated with a human face, around the head of which was a mural crown – that is a crown in the form of a city wall. All that survives of the Fishbourne vessel is part of the crown, but an almost identical pot is known from a villa at Rapsley in Surrey preserving, in addition, locks of hair projecting from beneath the crown. These vessels are not common and are best considered to be some kind of container for use during religious observances.

In the foregoing pages only a few of the hundreds of objects found have been mentioned, but together they give some idea of the complexity and style of life at Fishbourne from the late first to late third century. There is so much that we can never know, but future excavations may well provide some surprises.

Plate 71

XII

Fire and Destruction

Many times in the past it has been claimed that Roman buildings were destroyed by fire, without the evidence being sufficient to support the conclusion. At Fishbourne, however, there is no doubt: the inhabited part of the North Wing was enveloped by a disastrous fire which completely destroyed the superstructure of the building, leaving it a gutted ruin. The evidence is dramatic. Everywhere over the floor lay a thick blanket of broken and discoloured roof tiles, rafter nails and charred roof timbers, in some places lying in heaps up to a foot thick. A careful dissection of the rubble allowed further details of the process of collapse to be discovered. It appears that the roof was ablaze long enough for the lead fittings to melt and drip onto the mosaics, forming large puddles of the molten metal; then, the rafters weakened by the flames, the roof collapsed, some of the debris falling into the molten lead. The rafters continued to burn, discolouring the mosaics and tessellated floors with streaks of grey and blue, the heat being intense enough to refire completely the tiles from which the tesserae were made and occasionally to vitrify fragments of the roof tiles.

Plates 74, 75

Inside, the doors, door sills and timber partitions went up in flames. Several of the completely charred door sills still remain in position as witness to the fact and when the corridor in front of room N 7 was being excavated traces of its large doors were found where they had fallen forward. All that now remained were the iron strap hinges with the nails by which they were attached still in position, lying amidst the charcoal. In room N 11 the falling roof smashed the stacks of window panes and in many cases the heat was so intense that the glass melted and the panes buckled and contorted. One of them, which had been lying on an oyster shell, was so softened by the heat that it took up the shape of the shell.

Plate 76

The southern part of room N 12 was, at the time of the fire, used as a store room. Somewhere on its south wall was a shelf upon which had been placed a wooden box or tray, with its angles strengthened with iron bindings, a number of pots of normal kitchen wear and one large storage vessel containing a variety of lentils. The whole lot was completely

Plate 73

213

smashed by the falling roof, the individual sherds breaking apart and being refired by the heat from the burning rafters, so that when we stuck the pots together we found that normal black and grey coloured fragments joined to bright red pieces which had become oxidised in the flames.

All kinds of objects must have been lying about the building at the time, but only a few remained to be discovered. In the northern half of room N 12 a group of iron fittings had been left about, including a length of chain, a padlock and three iron hipposandals (a kind of horse-shoe). In room N 3 the remains of an axle were found, all that now survived being the iron axle-caps and the iron linchpins which kept the wheels in position. There must have been innumerable other fittings and objects, the furniture for example, none of which could have survived the blaze.

Immediately the flames had died down, people returned to the burnt out ruin. All the walls, with the exception of the one between rooms N 3 and 4, were still standing, many of them with their discoloured wall plaster still in position, but the roof must have completely gone and the floors were obscured beneath heaps of charred debris. Then the task of salvaging began. People raked carefully through the rubble taking away anything of value, including any complete roof tiles that may have survived. This much is clear from the nature of the rubble itself. The charred rafters had been churned up, and the roof tiles turned over so that fragments discoloured in an oxidising atmosphere were lying immediately next to those discoloured under reducing conditions. This could not have happened until after the fire had died down. Moreover not a single complete roof tile was found. Altogether the evidence of salvaging is clear.

One of the questions to arise is how far did the fire spread. As we shall see, the detached East Wing baths were not affected but the flames could easily have spread to the West Wing. Unfortunately the evidence here is not good, largely because the ploughing to which the area had been subjected in the Saxon and medieval periods removed most of the rubble. In those places where some rubble does survive, however, in the apse of the audience chamber and the basement of the hypocaust chamber, there is no trace of burning. On the other hand areas of discolouration appear on the mosaic in room N 8, a burnt door sill survives between rooms W 7 and 9, and in addition the painted plaster from the corridor behind the audience chamber has been badly scorched. On balance, then, it seems that the West Wing probably suffered burning but the absence of roof nails is puzzling, unless we suppose that part of the roof had been demolished or was being demolished in connection with the general rebuilding.

Plates 81, 82, 84

The baths in the East Wing escaped the flames because of their isolated position, but a bath building with no attached house was of very little value and the decision seems to have been taken to demolish it. First of all the suspended floors of the hypocaust were smashed up so that the useful pilae tiles and box tiles could be reached and the tiles, particularly the square ones of which the pilae were built, were systematically removed while the rubble and ash was shovelled out into neighbouring rooms. At this stage no attempt was made to dismantle the walls; it was the tiles which the salvagers were after.

The date at which the fire occurred can be defined within certain limits from the archaeological evidence. The pottery smashed by the collapse of the roof includes a number of coarseware types currently in use in the middle and latter part of the third century, while the finer wares are of types normally found in the late third and early fourth century. On this evidence a late third century date is indicated. Even greater precision is provided by the group of forty-three coins from the rubbish thrown out of the baths at the time of the demolition, all belonging to the period 270 to 296, the common issues of the early fourth century being completely absent. Therefore the post-fire demolition of the baths probably took place at the very end of the 290's. It is unlikely that we will ever be able to define the date more closely.

The burning of the building occured in a turbulent period of British history. [37] From the mid 280's Britain had been ruled as a breakaway state by the usurper Carausius, a marine who had originally been given the task of driving off the pirates then marauding along the Channel coasts. His enemies in Rome had accused him of being in league with the pirates, allowing them to land and pillage the coastal regions and then sharing their booty. This may have been so – at any event a return to Rome would probably have meant death, Carausius decided to make a stand, taking as his empire Britain and part of the Gaulish coast, centred on Boulogne. Although the Gaulish territory was soon lost, Carausius maintained his British empire and appears to have made many reforms, particularly to the coinage which was restored to a more stable basis, and there is some evidence of increasing prosperity in the towns and countryside. It was possibly in this new spirit that the rebuilding began at Fishbourne.

The murder of Carausius by his close supporter Allectus in 293 marked the beginning of growing unrest. Three years later, as the result of a carefully planned attack, the central Roman authorities led by Constantius Chlorus finally overran the breakaway province and restored it to the empire. The attack was a clear example of the vital importance of sea power to the defence of Britain. Constantius had divided his force into two: one arm, sailing west, outflanked the British fleet in the Channel and landed somewhere on the south coast. Marching inland they encountered Allectus and his army, composed of a large number of mercenaries, and soundly beat them. The other arm sailed along the Thames and arrived in London in time to stop the remnants of the beaten army from sacking the town. Britain was now safely restored to the Roman empire and the reverse of the famous gold medallion from Arras shows this event.

All this was happening whilst the final drama was being played out at Fishbourne. Some link between local and national events is not impossible. Undefended buildings close to the south coast would have been in some danger throughout much of the last thirty years of the century, but we cannot with any certainty assign the destruction of Fishbourne to the major events of recorded history. The fire could just as well have been caused by a careless workman as by the invading army of Constantius.

The return of Britain to Roman rule marked the beginning of a period of considerable prosperity. It was now that the villas began to reach their maximum size with all the luxuries of bath suites, central heating and elaborate mosaics. In the towns, too, there is evidence of widespread re-building. But at Fishbourne nothing remained except a fire-scarred ruin.

Why the villa was not rebuilt after the fire raises a number of interesting problems. After all, the masonry superstructure cannot have been badly damaged; minor repairs to the walls, complete reroofing and a re-plastering and painting would have restored the building quite adequately. But this was not done – instead the walls were systematically dismantled. It may be, of course, that the owner died in the fire but there is no evidence of this. On balance a more reasonable explanation would be that the natural environment was becoming hostile. We know that throughout the third century coastal regions of Britain were experiencing severe flooding as the result of a substantial rise in mean sea-level. [38] Estimates of between 15 and 20 ft have been made for some areas. The marsh was certainly encroaching on Fishbourne. By this stage much of the southern garden was permanently waterlogged, while to the north of the Palace spring water continued to be dammed up and here again marshy conditions were spreading over the made-up area which had previously been dry land. There was no simple solution to the problem, even large-scale drainage works would not have counteracted the flooding. While it is true that the marsh did not encroach upon the built-up area itself, the proximity of insect-infested swamps can hardly have been conducive to comfortable living. It is not difficult to visualize that day, towards the end of the third century, when the owner stood on the site and, looking from the burnt-out building to the encroaching marsh, finally made the decision to move elsewhere.

This did not mean the cessation of activity on the site. Far from it. The ruins were an extremely valuable source of building stone, particularly for the growing town of Chichester only a mile away. The fine ashlar masonry of the walls, the stylobate blocks and gutters and the columns would all have had a hard cash value in an area like this, where good building stone is hard to come by.

Plate 77

For some time after the fire the ruins were left standing, and under the effects of weathering plaster began to peel off the walls and accumulate in heaps, together with soil, over the collapsed roof. Evidently this process must have taken a period of a few years. Altogether the depth of rubble amounted to $2-2^{1}/_{2}$ ft. It was only after this period of neglect that robbing began and the walls were systematically demolished down to the flint cobble footings, which often lay 1–2 ft below the floor levels. The rubble left over after the usable building stone had been recovered was thrown back into the trenches and piled up in the rooms. The robbing was very precise below ground level and quite often the wall plaster, against the face of which the collapsed rubble had piled up, was still left in a vertical position after the stone of the wall had been removed. The plaster facing the west wall of room N1, for example, still remained in its original position, kept in place by the collapsed rubble inside the room and the thrown-back rubble in the robber trench behind. The robbing of the west wall of room N12 produced slightly different results. Here the painted plaster on both faces remained standing to a height of 2 ft whilst the wall was being robbed, but before the robber trench could be filled the plaster collapsed, first the west face and then the east. When this area was excavated it was possible to remove both layers of fallen plaster one after the other and to restore a section of them to their original positions.

An examination of the walls of the North Wing shows that, while most of them have been robbed to the flint footings, there are some sections which survived. Usually there is some explanation for this. In the case of the east end of the wing the reason is clear: the walls had been demolished to ground-level during the second century and nothing showed above ground by the time of the early fourth-century robbing to indicate the positions of the worthwhile remaining stone. At the west end of the wing the stone beneath the door sills usually remained untouched. After all, to get at it would have meant removing an overburden of 2–3 ft of rubble from the doorways and this was not considered to be worthwhile. Nor, apparently, was it considered to be worth the effort of removing up to 4 ft of collapsed building to reach the stylobate blocks and gutters buried deep in the north-west corner of the garden. Where the rubble cover was shallow however, away from the corner, everything was removed. Within the building the wall between rooms N3 and 4 still survived to a height of about 2 ft, but this was because the wall had collapsed during the fire and nothing remained above the general rubble level to give the stone robbers any idea that masonry survived just below.

The stones of the wall and the large stylobate blocks would have been re-usable in their original form but the gutter blocks were an awkward shape. Along the north side of the East Wing courtyard the individual slabs had been dragged out of position and the flanges knocked off and discarded before the rest of the block was carried away.

Systematic demolition on this scale must have taken a number of people some time to complete; many hundreds of tons of stone had to be loosened, cleaned, stacked, loaded and carted off. It seems that those engaged on the work probably camped for a while in the shell of the old East Wing, while the demolition of the North and West Wings was in progress. During this time a layer of occupation rubbish 6–9 ins thick accumulated on the floor of rooms E1–3, overlying the destroyed footings of the apse belonging to the *tepidarium*. It may be that the two hearths in room E2 belonged to this date, representing perhaps the place where the demolition gang ate and lived for the duration of the job. The pottery from that layer is the latest Roman ware to be found on the site, difficult to date with precision but assignable to the beginning of the fourth century – a date which fits well with the period during which the robbing is thought to have taken place. A few late coins dating to the first 20 years or so of the fourth century have been found scattered about the site, but they are very few indeed compared with the late third-century issues. Clearly by now occupation was at an end and when eventually, between AD 310–20, the last load of stone was removed and the demolition gang packed up and departed, they left behind them weed-covered heaps of rubble, with the old Palace garden long since overgrown and gone wild, and on both sides a gradually encroaching swamp. After 250 years of intensive occupation on a grand scale, nature was again taking over.

XIII

Aftermath

While Chichester flourished in the fourth century, Fishbourne passed from memory beneath a thickening mantle of soil, weather, worms, and plant growth combining to level out the contours of the now grass-grown heaps of rubble. At some later date in the sub-Roman or early Saxon period the site was used as a cemetery, for a group of at least four burials had been laid in graves cut down into the rubble of the old building. The absence of coffin nails or shroud pins leaves us ignorant as to the exact manner of burial but three of the bodies were laid on their backs in an extended position with their hands neatly folded over the pelvis in a manner clearly indicating careful burial. The fourth also lay on his back, but with knees flexed. Since three of the burials were orientated north-south, they are unlikely to be Christians and therefore some date in the immediate post-Roman period is suggested. More than this, it is impossible to say.

Plates 78, 79

The burials, like most of the rest of the site, were covered with a layer of grey soil containing finely broken-up mortar and rubble, representing a layer of ploughsoil created by long years of agricultural activity. Its thickness varied considerably from one part of the site to another, from a few inches over the West Wing to more than 3 ft thick immediately in front of it. Over the rather more level ground of the East Wing it averaged 18 ins. From this plough soil came a quantity of abraded potsherds ranging in date from the late Saxon period down to the sixteenth or seventeenth century with the characteristic green-glazed sherds of thirteenth or fourteenth century pitchers being the most common. The pottery must have come from kitchen and household refuse spread on the fields as manure derived from the houses of the medieval village of Fishbourne that was growing up on the promontory of land between the two inlets on either side of Mill Lane which leads down to the harbour. This area has produced a number of larger sherds of medieval pottery from the Mill Pond and also from the gardens of the modern houses. The site of the Roman palace had thus become the fields of a medieval peasant village.

Several coins of medieval and later date were found in the plough-soil, including a silver penny of Henry II or III, a groat of Henry VI and a half-groat of Henry VII or VIII. These too were probably brought out from the village in cartloads of manure.

The excavation of so large an area has led to the recognition of three of the medieval strip fields which had cut into the Roman floors of the West Wing, removing even the floor make-up in some areas, and leaving the edges of the ploughed areas sharply defined. It was because of this ploughing that so much of the West Wing was destroyed. The 15 ft wide baulks between the fields, which were left unploughed, have allowed strips of the original floors to survive and even larger areas remained intact beneath the headlands where the plough turned round at the end of each strip.

The strips were about 68 ft wide and probably a little over 400 ft long. No traces of continuous boundaries have been found between them, but a length of ditch marks the south side of one field and a ditch and three large pits were found in the baulk on the north side of another. The ditches probably result from attempts at draining particularly wet areas, while the pits might have been caused by tree growth along the boundary. The three fields cover much of the excavated areas, making it difficult to define the limits of agriculture, but fields may well have continued to the north up to the swampy area and at least one more field would have existed between the southernmost now recognizable and the line of the road. On the south side of the road some trace of medieval ploughing can be recognized but the proximity of the saltwater marsh would not have allowed width for more than a single strip.

While the West Wing was being ploughed the medieval farmers could hardly have failed to notice the flint footings of the Roman walls which would have caught the plough-share in a tiresome manner. Thus when flint was needed for building in the village the old ruin served to provide it. Several of the footings in the West Wing were completely removed at this time, as sherds of medieval pottery in the robber trenches show. Even one of the much deeper East Wing footings was robbed out for its flints. So deep was the robbing in all these cases that it can hardly have been simply to remove an obstruction to the plough. Indeed the ploughs were dragged through most of the intransigent soils, as the plough furrows carved through the clay of the garden and the mosaic in room N 13 show.

It is probable that the ploughing continued unabated until the time of the Enclosures in the eighteenth century, when the new larger fields were laid out with deep V-shaped ditches and thorn hedges – the boundaries which were still in existence when excavations began in 1961. It is hardly surprising that these new fields followed very closely the boundaries and alignments of those which they enclosed. It was during the eighteenth century that the village began to spread from its nucleus out along the south side of the road and eventually to the north side to where the house now known as 'The Bays' was built, together with its stable and yard which now cover the northern part of the proto-palace.

The nineteenth century saw the cessation of ploughing, allowing a rich stone-free topsoil to form which, sometime towards the middle of the century, was disturbed by a highly efficient system of land drainage constructed over the somewhat clayey area which had once been the formal Roman garden. Only a single pond was left towards the centre, not far from the pond which had been constructed during the 50's and 60's of the first century AD. The nineteenth-century pond continued in use until 1938, when piped water was laid to water troughs in the fields, one pipe miraculously missing four mosaic pavements by a matter of inches. It was at this time that the pond was filled with soil and when it was re-excavated in 1966 in connection with the examination of the Roman garden, the hoof marks of the last few cows who drank from it in the summer of 1938 could still be recognized. They were, needless to say, photographed in accordance with normal archaeological practice.

By 1960 the village had grown considerably, spreading out in all directions from its old nucleus, and it was only the discovery and subsequent purchase of the site of the Palace that prevented it, too, from being engulfed by modern housing development and becoming a suburb of Chichester.

We have ended where we began, for after all the past is continuously being created. But what of the future? So far we have excavated all of the Palace at present available for excavation together with the early levels preceding it, but this is only a fraction of Roman Fishbourne. Barely six months before these words were written the harbour area with its enormous archaeological potential was discovered to the south, on land, much of which can be excavated. But excavation of these waterlogged deposits will be difficult, involving coffer-dams and continuous pumping while the conservation of the organic material which will inevitably be found will require specially designed vacuum impregnation units – all this will be expensive and will require detailed planning. An easier problem will be raised when the trunk road is diverted across the land immediately to the east side of the site, sometime within the next decade. And then there are the problems of the Palace estate and its layout, problems which are now gradually being tackled by aerial photography and ground survey.

Much, then, remains to be done. We cannot say that future excavation at Fishbourne will be as spectacular as that of the last nine years, but it is going to be every bit as fascinating.

Notes

CHAPTER I

1   T.W. Horsfield, *The History, Antiquities, and Topography of the County of Sussex*, Lewes 1835, II, 52.

2   *Gentleman's Magazine*, 1805 (ii), 926–7.

3   *Hampshire Telegraph and Sussex Chronicle*, Monday, April 7, 1806, p. 2, col. 3.

4   *The Times* (correspondence), February 11, 1929.

5   Interim reports were published in the *Antiquaries Journal* at the end of each season's excavation. *Ant. Journ.* XLII (1962) 15–23; XLIII (1963) 1–14; XLIV (1964) 1–8; XLV (1965) 1–11; XLVI (1966) 26–38; XLVII (1967) 51–59; XLVIII (1968) 32–40.
    A short summary appeared in *Antiquity* XXXIX (1965), 177–183. A full report has been published by the Society of Antiquaries of London: B.W. Cunliffe, *The Roman Palace at Fishbourne: Excavations 1961–9*, vols I and II, London 1971.

CHAPTER II

6   R. Bradley, The Chichester Entrenchments, in B.W. Cunliffe, *The Roman Palace at Fishbourne, Excavations 1961–9*, vol. I, 17–36.

7   Conveniently summarized in S.S. Frere, *Britannia*, London 1967, 39–60.

8   Cassius Dio, *History of the Romans*, Book LX.

9   For a summary see B.W. Cunliffe (*ed.*), *Fifth Report on the Excavations of the Roman Fort at Richborough, Kent*, London 1968, 231–41.

10 Tacitus, *Agricola* 14.

11 *RIB*. 91.

12 Tacitus, *Annals* XI, 14 ff.

CHAPTER III

13 Hans Schönberger, Augusteisches Lager Rödgen, *Saalburg-Jahrbuch* XXI (1963–4), 95–108.

14 I.A. Richmond, *Hod Hill*, vol. 2 (London 1968), fig. 46A.

15 Suetonius, *Vespasian*.

16 Tacitus, *Agricola* 25.

CHAPTER IV

17 *RIB*. 92.

18 S.S. Frere, Excavations at Verulamium, 1958, *Antiquaries Journal* XXXIX (1959), fig. 3.

CHAPTER V

19 J.B. Ward Perkins and J.M.C. Toynbee, The Hunting Baths at Lepcis Magna, *Archaeologia* XCIII (1949), 165–95.

20 L. Scott, The Roman Villa at Angmering, *Sussex Archaeological Collections* 79 (1938), 3–44.

21 For general notes on these villas, see *VCH. Sussex* III.

CHAPTER VI

22 Domitian's palace is conveniently described in W.L. MacDonald, *The Architecture of the Roman Empire*, Yale 1965, 47–74.

23 MacDonald, *ibid.* fig. 40.

24 For Richborough see B.W. Cunliffe (*ed.*), *Fifth Report on the Excavation of the Roman Fort at Richborough, Kent*, London 1968, 241 and fig. 29; for Silchester see *Archaeologia* LIV, 222 ff.

CHAPTER VII

25 Pliny, *Letters*, Book II, letter 17.

26 Pliny, *Letters*, Book V, letter 6.

27 Both of Pliny's letters on the subject are worth reading, letter 17 in Book II and letter 6 in Book V.

CHAPTER VIII

28 Tacitus, *Agricola*, 21.

29 Tacitus, *Agricola*, 14.

30 *RIB.* 91.

31 S.S. Frere, *Britannia*, London 1967, 83.

CHAPTER IX

32 A very useful account of the development of mosaic art in Britain with some reference to Fishbourne is given in D.J. Smith, The Mosaic Pavements, in A.L.F. Rivet, *The Roman Villa in Britain*, London 1969, 71–126.

33 R.E.M. and T.V. Wheeler, *Verulamium: a Belgic and two Roman Cities*, London 1936, pl. XXXIX.

CHAPTER XI

34 E.g. J. Liversidge, *Britain in the Roman Empire*, London 1968.

35 Pliny, *Nat. Hist.*

36 A summary of the documentary evidence occurs in J. Lawson, The Roman Garden, *Greece and Rome* xix (1950), 97–105.

CHAPTER XII

37 See S.S. Frere, *Britannia*, London 1967, 335–46, for a general discussion of the background.

38 B.W. Cunliffe, The Somerset Levels in the Roman Period, in A.C. Thomas (*ed.*), *Rural Settlement in Roman Britain*, London 1966, 68–73.

List of Illustrations

Unless otherwise acknowledged the photographs are by David Baker and published by permission of the Fishbourne Excavation Committee of the Chichester Civic Society.
The maps and plans are based on the original excavation drawings by the author, adapted by David Eccles. Reconstruction drawings numbers 4, 9 and 35 are by Nigel Sunter, number 30 by David S. Neal.

Colour Plates

Monochrome Plates

226

Index